Tricker's Water Gardening Book

An Introduction and Guide

By Richard Lee
President
William Tricker, Inc.
Independence, Ohio

All rights reserved. No part of this book may be reproduced in any form or by any means, electronic or mechanical, including photocopying, recording or by any information storage and retrieval system without written permission from the author or publisher.

The development of this book was based on the experience and knowledge of the author with input from numerous resources. The information contained herein is true and complete to the best of the author's knowledge and is not intended to promote the violation of any laws or statutes.

Some aquatic plants can be or are considered extremely invasive or noxious by specific states. Reputable distributors of such aquatic plants should alert you of this status and may refuse or may be unable to send specfic aquatic plants to a state due to such restrictions.

© 1996 by William Tricker, Inc.

Illustrations: Anastasia Higgins
Design and Typography: Cindy Ludrosky
Photography: William Tricker, Inc.

Published and distributed by: William Tricker, Inc.
7125 Tanglewood Drive
Independence, Ohio 44131
(216) 524-3491

ISBN 0-9649814-0-8

Tricker's Water Gardening Book

An Introduction and Guide

CONTENTS

Preface: History of Aquatic Culture & William Tricker, Inc 4

Chapter 1: How to make a Water Garden Pool 7

Chapter 2: Water Lilies and Victoria 12

Chapter 3: Lotus 25

Chapter 4: Shallow Water and Bog Plants 29

Chapter 5: Floating and Oxygenating Plants 39

Chapter 6: Fish in the Water Garden Pool 43

Chapter 7: Scavengers 53

Chapter 8: Miscellaneous Water Garden Topics 56
    Water Fountains and Cascades, Filters: Biological and Mechanical, Overfill Drains, Stray Animals, Cement Cracks, Algae and Fall Preparation.

Chapter 9: Arranging the Water Plants in the Pool and Tub Gardens 61

PREFACE

HISTORY of AQUATIC CULTURE and WILLIAM TRICKER, INC.

Who would ever have thought that over 100 years ago the hard work and efforts of a single individual, William Tricker, would still be enjoyed today in our water gardens. We at William Tricker, Inc., Independence, Ohio are extremely proud to carry on a tradition that began so long ago with the company started by William Tricker himself.

There are many important individuals that have contributed to the historical development of America's oldest water garden specialist William Tricker, Inc. and it would be most appropriate to mention a few contributors: William Tricker, Charles Tricker, Albert Buskirk, W.G. O'Brien, Robert V. Sawyer, Charles O. Master, W. Schmidlin, Gilbert Lambacher and Dr. J. T. Charleson.

WILLIAM TRICKER and W.G. O'BRIEN:

William Tricker (1852-1916) formally known as Charles William Bret Tricker, was a water lily pioneer and originated commercial water lily culture. He began to hybridize water lilies in the 1890's and was considered a world authority on water plants. In the early 1890's he began to send out his water lily hybrids from Clifton, N.J. and later built aquatic greenhouses in Arlington, N. J. Many articles on aquatics appeared in the literature in the 1890's by William Tricker. Some of his best hybrids are still known and sold in the water lily trade today around the world. His first commercial water lily catalog was produced in 1895 and he wrote the first American specialized aquatic text *The Water Garden,* published in 1897. This book is considered a master piece and the first attempt at informing the gardener growing aquatics in the water garden throughout the world. He later wrote another text, *Making a Water Garden* published in 1913.

William Tricker
1852-1916
Founder of Wm. Tricker, Inc.

In the later 1800's rock quarrying came to an end in Independence, Ohio. The abandoned rock quarry left behind springs, streams, lakes and ponds which were to become a part of the William Tricker company as we know it today.

At the turn of the 19th century in Independence, Ohio a horticulturist and businessman by the name of Albert Buskirk (1874-1953) had greenhouses built that would support a branch of aquatic plants and fish raising, which was a part of Independence Nurseries. The supporting springs and ponds from the old abandoned 1800's rock quarry would make this a perfect spot for aquatic development and the future site of William Tricker, Inc. Albert Buskirk also became known for hybridizing water lilies and received awards for his efforts.

William G. O'Brien (1889-1927), a chemical engineer from Akron, Ohio was selected to continue to develop, expand and operate the aquatic and fish raising branch at Independence Nurseries. W.G. O'Brien was a noted aquarist and hybridist who was recognized nationally from his published articles on aquatics and fish topics.

It was through the efforts of W.G. O'Brien that formally merged the aquatic branch of Independence Nurseries with the William Tricker company of Arlington, N.J. Both of these companies had already established a reputation in aquatics and were well known nationally to aquatic lovers. After years of determination and cooperation, the merger

William G. O'Brien
1889-1928

was formally completed and in 1927 was incorporated in the state of Ohio as William Tricker, Inc.

Besides being credited with creating hybrid water lilies and developing new breeds of fish, W.G. O'Brien made history when he discovered the first aquatic "*pH test kit*" that is used around the world. It was through his effort that testing the water for pH has become a common occurrence in aquariums and water gardens around the world.

MEMORIALS: Monuments in Time

At the time of Mr. W.G. O'Brien's accidental death in 1928 the aquarist across the nation were in shock. He was extremely well known as a leader in the industry. The main building of William Tricker, Inc. was dedicated to Mr. O'Brien in 1928 after his death and displays the original plaque. Thus, we have a standing monument of his contributions.

William Tricker's memory re-lives each year as our catalog carrying his name is delivered to our customers. His wonderful hybrids bloom and grow in our greenhouses waiting to bring another year of enjoyment to water gardeners around the world.

On September 1, 1928 a photograph from inside one of our aquatic greenhouses at Independence, Ohio was shown in a trade magazine, *The Florist Exchange,* and commented:

"If the late William Tricker could come back today, how overwhelmed he would be with the progress of the firm which he started so soundly and took such merited pride in. What finer monument could there be to his lovable nature and sterling character."

This same historic greenhouse is still standing today at William Tricker, Inc. The foundation of this greenhouse is made of sandstone from the old 1800's rock quarry and still uses the original spring water coming from the quarry to produce some of the finest water lilies today; a true standing monument to William Tricker and the company he started so long ago.

FINAL COMMENTS:

William Tricker wrote in his 1897 text *The Water Garden* in his preface:

> "**If this add in any way to the better appreciation of the beauties of the Water Garden and its charming occupants; if it lead but a few towards that great pleasure and satisfaction which has been mine after years of experiment and trial, the labor of production will not have been in vain. "**
> William Tricker   1897

It is with this statement that the mission of the William Tricker company commits to continue to provide the finest aquatics in the world for all to enjoy in water gardening. Therefore, the labor of production in aquatics of William Tricker will not be in vain as we will enter another century.

Richard Lee
President
William Tricker, Inc.

CHAPTER 1

How to Make a Water Garden Pool:

Historically many water garden pools were made of concrete. In 1909 an eight foot by four foot water garden pool could be made by a professional mason for $11.28, including the water pipes and drains. It is not unusual to find these historic water gardens growing water lilies today. Concrete water gardens are still made today, however lesser expensive methods are available that do not require a professional mason.

Most holes dug in the ground will not hold water due to seepage into the soil. Therefore a method to resist the water from seeping into the ground is necessary in making a water garden pool. Besides concrete two types of water gardening material is available: *POOL LINERS* or *PREFORMED POOLS*. Before selecting a material, the site must be considered.

I. SITE LOCATION:

Before a hole is dug for the water garden pool a good location should be selected. Many criteria must be taken in consideration of this location for the water garden pool and hope that the expression *"I should have put the water garden pool over there"* is never said.

1. **View of the water garden.** Some water gardeners prefer to locate the water garden to be in view from inside the home

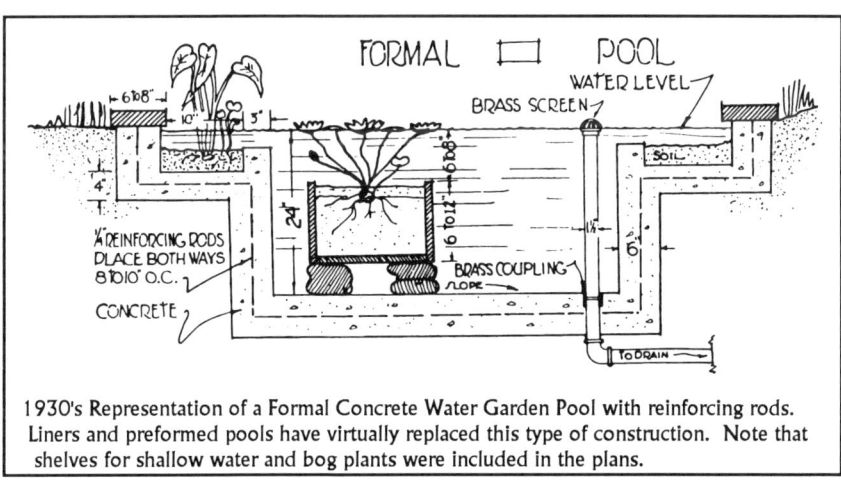

1930's Representation of a Formal Concrete Water Garden Pool with reinforcing rods. Liners and preformed pools have virtually replaced this type of construction. Note that shelves for shallow water and bog plants were included in the plans.

through a window. Others prefer to find a secluded spot that is nested in some special location on the property that is discovered during each trip to the garden.

2. **Electrical/Water access.** The location of the water garden must have access to a water supply. If a waterfall, fountain or lights are to be added, the water garden must also have electricity available.

3. **Sunlight.** The majority of water garden plants need at least three to four hours of direct sunlight. Thus, the path of the sun during the entire growing season must be taken into consideration. Large trees that may not shade the selected spot in April may totally shade the location in August. Trees also shed their leaves and often become a nuisance in the Autumn.

4. **Runoff Rain Water.** The water garden is best to be at the highest location on the property. This will prevent runoff water from rain that may contain pesticides, herbicides, etc. from entering the water garden pool. Provisions should be made if the location is not at the highest point. The edge of the pond should be made slightly higher than the surrounding area. This will redirect the runoff rain water away from the water garden. This slight raise is often not noticeable. [Note: Sometimes runoff water may accumulate under a liner pond. Redirecting the water away from the water garden prevents this from occurring.]

II. POOL LINERS:

Pool liners are made of a durable rubber or PVC (Polyvinylchloride) and must be fish and plant safe. The color of the liner is black which will give the maximum reflection in the water and hide the liner. Since the liner will be exposed to damaging ultraviolet light, the liner must resist this type of weathering. The rubber pool liner is often the first choice by the vast majority of water gardeners. The rubber liner is more flexible, can resist tears and will give many more years of satisfaction than a PVC liner.

Virtually any shape can be made using a liner. The water garden pool should be approximately two feet deep and not less than one and a half foot deep.

ESTIMATING THE SIZE OF THE LINER:

Since the liners are sheets in squares or rectangles, draw a square or rectangle around the design made for the water garden.

Measure the length (ft) and width (ft) of the pool desired. Add twice the pool's depth to each dimension plus an allowance of one foot for overlap at the edges. For example, a 5 foot X 10 foot, 2 foot deep pool requires a liner:

WIDTH: 5' + 4' (twice the depth)
        + 1' (overlap) = 10 feet

LENGTH: 10 '+ 4 '(twice the depth)
        + 1' (overlap) = 15 feet

Thus, in this example the liner required would be 10 feet by 15 feet.

INSTALLATION OF THE POOL LINER:

STEP 1. GARDEN DESIGN: The garden pool need not exceed 18 to 24 inches in depth. Lay out your design on the ground that will contain your garden pool. A rubber hose or length of rope can outline the pool on the ground.

Lay out the design before digging

STEP 2. DIGGING: Dig to the desired depth. The sides can be sloped if desired. Check the depth by placing a board that is **level** across the top and use a yardstick to measure the depth. Any added height to make the board level at one end should

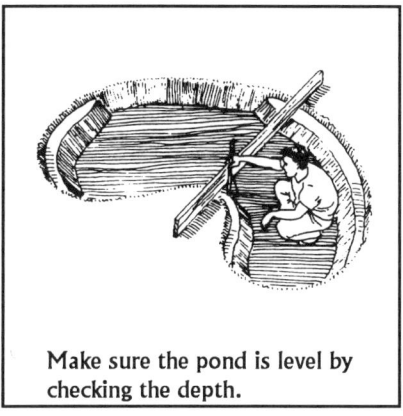

Make sure the pond is level by checking the depth.

be added to the proposed depth. Thus, if two inches were necessary to make the board level at one end, add this two inches to the desired digging depth.

STEP 3. LEDGES AND PREPARATION: A ledge can be added for bog plants. The ledge can be 9 to 12 inches wide and at least 6 inches below the rim on one or more sides of the pool. Remove all protruding stones or roots in the pool. To cover irregularities and cushion the liner under considerable weight of water, line the hole with an inch thick of sand. A mat of old newspapers or a old rug can be used to line the bottom of the hole.

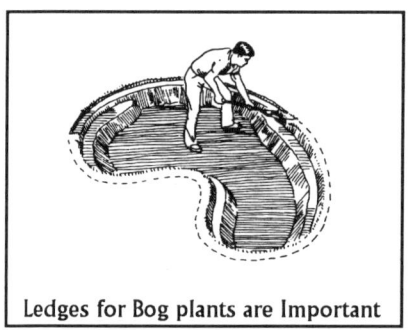
Ledges for Bog plants are Important

STEP 4. POOL LINER PLACEMENT. Open the pool liner and place it over the dug hole. Spread it across the hole so that it overlaps evenly on all sides. Secure the liner in place by holding down the edges with bricks or smooth stones.

CAUTION: DO NOT CUT OR TRIM THE LINER UNTIL THE POOL IS COMPLETELY FILLED WITH WATER. SEE STEP 5.

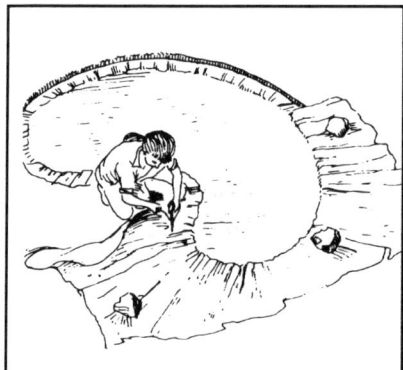
Caution: Do not cut or trim the liner until the pool is completely filled with water.

STEP 5. FILLING AND COMPLETING THE WATER GARDEN. Fill the pool with your water source. If you must walk on the liner, it is best to go barefoot or wear sneakers to avoid accidental tears or punctures. After the pool is full, it is best to wait a couple of days until everything settles before trimming off the excess liner with a pair of large scissors, leaving at least a 6 to 8 inch flap around the edges. The flap can then be covered with edging stones, paving blocks, or bricks. If your water is chlorinated you have to wait at least 24 hours or add an antichlorine agent if you intend to add fish or scavengers.

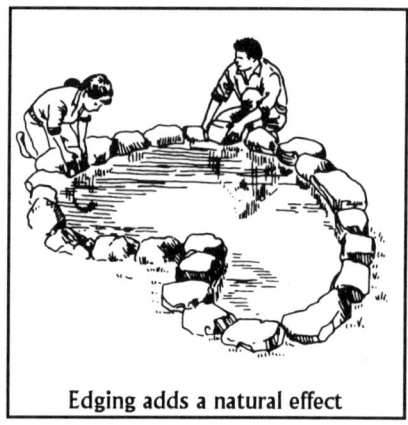
Edging adds a natural effect

III. PREFORMED POOLS.

Preformed pools are often made of durable polyethylene. Preformed fiberglass pools were prone to cracking and have been replaced by this durable polyethylene. They are light weight with shelves for bog plants and are very easy to install. But just as important as with the liner, the preformed pool must be installed level.

STEP 1. OUTLINING THE HOLE. After selecting a site for installation lay the preformed pool on the ground upright. Mark the shape of the hole to be dug. This can be done by placing stakes around the edge of the preformed pool or lying a garden hose or rope around the shape.

Preformed Pools are easy to install and come in many shapes and sizes

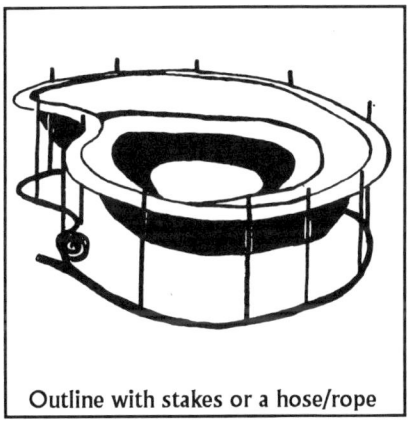

Outline with stakes or a hose/rope

STEP 2. DIGGING THE HOLE. The hole should be dug the shape outlined. It is very important for the bottom to be level. Dig the depth of the preformed pool and add approximately one inch for the sand. If you are adding a stone edge, allow the additional depth of stones. Make sure the bottom is well compacted and spread about one inch of sand over the bottom. Check the depth by placing a board that is **level** across the top and use a yardstick to measure the depth. See page 9, STEP 2 with illustration.

STEP 3. PLACING THE PREFORMED POOL IN THE HOLE. After the hole is dug, place the preformed pool into the hole. Remove it and observe the impression in the sand. The preformed pool must be fully supported and imprinted in the sand. Add more sand if necessary in low spots.

STEP 4. FILLING THE PREFORMED POOL. Backfill the sides of the preformed pool. Begin filling the pool with water, checking periodically to check to make sure the pool is level. If the water is chlorinated and you intend to introduce fish or scavengers, wait at least 24 hours or add an antichlorine agent.

CHAPTER 2

WATER LILIES and VICTORIA.

The water lilies are often the focus of the water garden pool. They have a beauty unequaled in the plant world.

There are two main groups of water lilies: *TROPICAL WATER LILIES* and *HARDY WATER LILIES*. Each group has its own special desirable characteristics. In choosing a water lily for a water garden pool many criteria should be considered.

General Characteristic	Tropical Water Lily	Hardy Water Lily
Aroma	Strongly Aromatic	Slight to No Aroma
Number of Flowers	Many Flowers per Plant	Single to Many Flowers
Location of Flowers	Flowers Held on Stems above the water	Flowers Float on water surface
Color of Flowers	All Colors	No blue or purple shades
Night Bloomers	Many Varieties	None
Mottled Lily Pads	Many Varieties light to strongly mottled	Varieties light to medium mottled
Wintering	Can be wintered, however treated as Annual. Will continue to bloom until frost.	Perennial, plant tuber prepares for winter, reduces flower production before frost.
Viviparous Leaf	Many Varieties	None

The naming of the water lilies are often the privilege of the person who hybridized or introduced the water lily. Quite often the names of the water lilies reflect individuals that were important at the time of introduction or a descriptive characteristic of the new water lily. Botanically water lilies discussed are in the genus *Nymphaea*. For example, the correct botanical term for the water lily *BLUE BEAUTY* would be *Nymphaea 'Blue Beauty'*.

There is a special group of water lilies known as *pygmy* water lilies, of which are found in both the hardy and tropical varieties. The flowers and water lily pads are smaller in size. They are especially desired in the small water gardens or tub gardens.

I. TROPICAL WATER LILIES.

INTRODUCTION. The beauty of the tropical water lily is unrivaled in the plant kingdom, including the hardy variety water lily. The tropical water lily offers many more desirable growing characteristics than the hardy varieties. Unlike the need for special arrangements or provisions in Europe and England the weather in the United States is extremely favorable for growing tropical water lilies. It is no doubt that many of our delightful tropical water lily hybrids have originated in the United States and have remained for decades. With this in mind the stage is set to discuss one of Nature's most wonderful plants, the tropical water lilies.

FLOWERS OF THE TROPICAL WATER LILIES. The flowers of the tropical water lilies represent every color of the rainbow: blues, purples, autumn shades, pinks, whites, yellows and reds. Unlike some flowers that bloom for a few weeks in a growing season, the tropical water lilies will bloom continually all summer. Each flower will last approximately three days, often showing different shades of color each day, some intensifying or some lessening in color depending upon the variety.

The tropical water lily will bloom profusely during the summer and it is not unusual to have several blooms at one time on a single plant. The blooms on long slender stems are held high above the water surface and can be seen from a distant. The flower and stem held high above the water makes a reflection in the water that is most pleasing and attractive. A gentle breeze will create a peaceful sway of the flower giving a busy bumble bee a memorable ride as he enjoys the sweet enchanting nectar of a tropical water lily.

FRAGRANCES OF THE TROPICAL WATER LILIES. The fragrance of the tropical water lily is delightful. Many tropical water lilies have distinct different aromas. They make excellent cut flowers and can be brought indoors and placed in a vase or floated in a dish of water. Not only a wonderful sight but the aroma that fills the air can be enjoyed by all.

MOTTLED LILY PADS OF THE TROPICAL WATER LILIES. Some varieties of tropical water lilies have intensely marked variegation in the water lily pad commonly known as "mottled lily pads." This mottling is superior over the hardy varieties of water lilies. The summer heat can diminish any deep colored mottling in hardy water lilies, but since the tropical water lilies thrive in heat the mottled lily pads remain as a beautiful sight during the entire summer.

VIVIPAROUS TROPICAL WATER LILIES. Some varieties of tropical water lilies have a characteristic of being "viviparous", or producing a new plant from the center of the water lily pad.

After a floating viviparous water lily pad becomes mature, the area where the petal and stem attach a small dark colored swelling develops. After a few days this swelling develops into a small plant. As roots begin to develop, the small plantlet can be removed from the leaf and replanted. This small miniature plant will be able to grow into a new tropical water lily, a very fascinating and unusual trait.

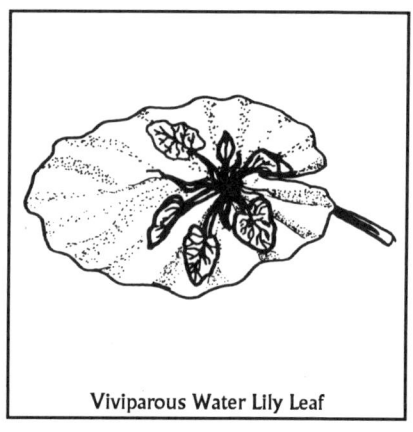

Viviparous Water Lily Leaf

GROWING CHARACTERISTICS OF TROPICAL WATER LILIES. Tropical water lilies are extremely easy to grow. They not only grow fast but transplant well. The weather in the United States is favorable for growing tropical water lilies in outdoor water gardens without special provisions. Once planted outside they will begin to flourish immediately.

DAY OR NIGHT BLOOMING VARIETIES OF TROPICAL WATER LILIES. The flowers of water lilies, hardy or tropical, do not stay open continually during a single bloom. Most gardeners are familiar with the open water lily flower as seen in the afternoon. Unknown to many of us is that late in the afternoon the flower will close for the night. This is typical of all hardy water lilies, however the tropical water lily surprises us in having two categories of blooming characteristics. There are varieties that will open their flowers in the early morning and close in the late afternoon, known *day bloomers,* and varieties that will open their flowers in the late afternoon and close in the day, known as *night bloomers.* This wonderful blooming characteristic allows the water gardener to enjoy blooms 24 hours a day by mixing the tropical day bloomers with tropical night bloomers.

The night blooming water lily is an aggressive and strong growing water lily. The night blooming flowers will begin to open as the day blooming water lily flowers close for the night. The color of the flower seen at dusk is often transformed into a mystic color in moonlight or artificial light. Water gardeners that work in the day will often come home and enjoy the beauty of the night blooming tropical in the evening even though the day blooming water lilies are closed. It is this very reason that many water gardeners will grow both day bloomers and night bloomers to enjoy 24 hours of water lily blooms.

HYBRID TROPICAL WATER LILIES:

The William Tricker company of Independence, Ohio has introduced and hybridized many new and exciting tropical water lilies originating as far back as the early 1890's.

Tropical Water Lily *Mrs. Robert Sawyer* The first pink water lily of the viviparous type hybridized at William Tricker, Inc.

Due to our favorable weather in the United States, William Tricker (1854-1916) believed that tropical water lilies should be a part of everyone's water garden. William Tricker began hybridizing tropical water lilies in the early 1890's. Many of William Tricker's tropical water lily hybrids were introduced through his company, William Tricker and Company. After his death in 1916 the mission of the William Tricker company was to continue to provide and discover new tropical water lily hybrids. Throughout the decades that followed William Tricker's death many noteworthy hybridizers were employed at the William Tricker company and produced many fine hybrid tropical water lilies. Such contributors included R.V. Sawyer, G. Lambacher, A. Buskirk, J.T. Charleston and W.G. O'Brien. The hybrids produced are a tribute to William Tricker who had shown us the beauty of the tropical water lily.

Many other water lily hybridizers followed in the path of William Tricker and produced other new and unique tropical water lilies for our enjoyment. Dr. George Pring (1885-1969), superintendent of the Missouri Botanical Garden at St. Louis, experimented with and hybridized the tropical water lilies. He discovered many new and exciting hybrids which were all introduced through the William Tricker Company.

SPECIAL VARIETIES OF TROPICAL WATER LILIES.

The following is a list of the Tropical Water Lilies directly hybridized and introduced by the William Tricker company and are currently being offered today. These represent a history of over 100 years of selection of the finest tropical water lilies and a pride of the company William Tricker, Inc:

BLUE TROPICAL WATER LILIES:

Blue Beauty. *Blue Beauty* is a special hybrid developed by William Tricker and has been a number one seller among the tropical water lilies. Blossoms are deep blue, have a spicy fragrance, and stand six to eight inches above the water surface. Leaves or pads are dark green and slightly speckled with brown above and beneath the leaves. The margins of the leaf are wavy with lobes long and tapering. In spite of its potential size the water lily does well in tub gardens or small pools.

Blue Beauty

Mrs. Woodrow Wilson. This tropical is a beautiful William Tricker hybrid derived from *N. Dauben* and bears the same leaf characteristics of being viviparous. This variety is a much stronger grower than Dauben and produces lavender-blue flowers of much greater size.

Colonel Lindbergh. This tropical water lily was developed by William Tricker and was referred to as "Lindy." The blossoms are large and very dark blue with wide petals and a delightful fragrance. The flowers are held high above the water surface and have attractive mottled pads.

Blue Bird. This hybrid was developed by William Tricker and has deep blue colored blossoms which are extremely plentiful all summer long. The plant reproduces viviparously and was named after the Blue Bird which will bring good luck.

William Stone. This tropical was originated by William Tricker and has particularly attractive violet-blue blossoms. The blossoms are held high above the water and are star-shaped and open early in the morning and do not close until late afternoon.

Shirley Ann. This tropical was originated at William Tricker, Inc. and a hybrid of Mr. Charleston and Mr. Lambacher. This is an outstanding blue water lily that is a very strong grower and produces many beautiful blossoms all summer long.

PURPLE TROPICAL WATER LILIES:

Panama Pacific. William Tricker introduced this outstanding viviparous hybrid in honor of the 1914 Panama Pacific Exposition in the United States. The blossoms are a brilliant wine red that bleeds into a reddish purple. The buds are attractive and the flowers are extremely fragrant.

Royal Purple. This tropical was originated at William Tricker, Inc. and a hybrid of Albert Buskirk. Considered a pygmy water lily with royal purple blossoms and golden yellow stamens. It is a moderate grower and desired in small to large water gardens.

PINK TROPICAL WATER LILIES:

Mrs. C.W. Ward. This tropical was produced by William Tricker and has large blossoms with pointed rose pink petals. The stamens are golden yellow tipped with pink. The flowers are held about 15 inches above the water level.

Independence. This beautiful hybrid was developed at William Tricker, Inc. by Robert Sawyer and named after the small city of Independence, Ohio, the location of William Tricker, Inc. The blossoms are rich pink and extremely abundant. The plant is viviparous.

Royal Purple

Independence

Mrs. Robert Sawyer. This is the first pink viviparous water lily and was hybridized by Robert Sawyer. The water lily has gorgeous full petaled flowers.

Rose Marie. A cross developed at William Tricker, Inc. between the water lily *Mrs. Robert Sawyer* and the water lily *Dauben* resulted in the hybrid "Rose Marie". The plant is viviparous and has petals of deep pink and pointed.

Cleveland. This hybrid was developed at William Tricker, Inc. and named in honor of the close proximity of William Tricker, Inc. to Cleveland, Ohio. The blossoms are rose-pink with slightly pointed petals and has beautiful mottled pads.

Trickeri. This tropical night bloomer was developed by William Tricker. The leaves glisten emerald green above and dark brown beneath. The blossoms are pink suffused with white.

Charles Tricker. This tropical night bloomer was developed by William Tricker and he named this wonderful hybrid after his son who later ran the business after his death. The blossoms are large and magenta-red in color and are produced in great numbers.

Delicatissma. This tropical night bloomer was developed by William Tricker. The leaves are slightly crumpled around the margins and have a metallic luster on the upper surface. The pink color of the blossoms is a very "delicate" pink.

Patricia. This is an extremely wonderful hybrid that was developed at William Tricker, Inc. by Mr. W.G. O'Brien. It was named after his wife who had auburn hair. The lily is considered a pygmy due to the small crimson flowers and pale-green leaves. The plant is viviparous.

WHITE TROPICAL WATER LILIES:

Alice Tricker. This tropical was introduced by William Tricker, Inc. and is considered an improved white tropical water lily. It has large blossoms with wide petals and is a strong grower.

Alice Tricker

Janice. This hybrid was the first white viviparous tropical water lily. It was introduced at William Tricker, Inc. and hybridized by Mr. Robert Sawyer. *Janice* has an exquisite pure white flower that is bell-shaped with many yellow stamens.

PLANTING TROPICAL WATER LILIES.
Tropical water lilies in the latitude of Chicago, Cleveland and New

York should not be put outside until the first week of June when the water warms and the temperatures are around 70 degrees Fahrenheit. After June the tropical water lilies can be planted at anytime during the summer months. Southern states can place the tropical water lily out sooner.

Since the tropical water lily grows rapidly, within a few weeks the plant will appear as if it has been growing for months. Tropical water lilies that were grown in pots transplant exceptionally well due to the limited damage or disturbance to the root system.

The water lily received in the mail is wrapped in wet paper inside a plastic bag. The sooner the planting of the water lily the better. The plant should be immediately unwrapped and planted. If a delay in planting is expected, float the water lily in water and cover the roots with paper to protect from the sun.

Selecting a suitable potting container size depends upon the expected growth. The water lily, as with many plants, will characteristically grow in relationship to the size of the planting container. That is, the larger the planting container the larger the water lily pads, flowers, etc.

Follow these simple five steps in planting a water lily:

STEP 1. Fill the selected potting container with a good topsoil. Do not use commercial potting soil. Mix one pound of fertilizer, *Praefecta*™, with three bushels of soil. *Praefecta*™ is a proven granular fertilizer developed for aquatic plants at William Tricker, Inc. by one of their chemical engineers. Do not over fertilize. A common sign of over fertilization is the lily pads immediately dying and turning brown with subsequent death of the plant turning to mush.

STEP 2. Hollow out a planting hole with your hands.

STEP 3. Hold the water lily in position and bury the roots with additional soil.

STEP 4. Sprinkle a half-inch layer of sand or pea gravel over the top of the soil. This will keep the soil in place when the container is submerged under water.

STEP 5. Slowly sink the potted container with lily into your water garden five to six inches below the water surface. If necessary, use bricks or stones to elevate the container to the correct height.

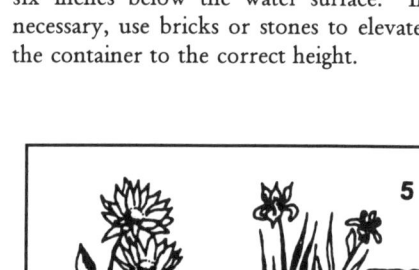

Tropical Water Lily placed in Pool

CARE OF THE TROPICAL WATER LILY.

Fertilizing is necessary to keep the water lily blooming and growing. *Trico*™, a hard pellet of aquatic fertilizer, can be poked into the soil next to the roots of the water lily once a month.

If aphids appear, they can be easily washed off with a strong spray of water from a garden hose. If your water garden pool has fish, these aphids become a real treat.

It is best to consider the tropical water lily as an annual, unless one has the advantage of a greenhouse. The hours and months of the true enjoyment from a single growing season with a tropical water lily lasts a lifetime. There are many wonderful tropical water lily hybrids that can be enjoyed each season.

II. Hardy Water Lilies.

INTRODUCTION. Hardy water lilies often provide the water garden pool with years of beauty. The flowers come in all colors except the shades of blues, purples or greens which are found in the tropical water lilies.

HYBRID HARDY WATER LILY.

Many of the beautiful and unusual hybrids are from the achievement of a Frenchman, Bory Latour-Marliac (1830-1911) and are commonly known as *Marliac hybrids*. One of William Tricker company's early noted hybridist and author Robert Sawyer commented in his text that *"Marliac crossed and recrossed the various hardy water lilies varieties back and forth until they hardly knew themselves."* Since there are no blue or purple shades of flowers in hardy water lilies, one would wonder if Marliac would have produced these colors if he would have lived longer.

In 1894 an individual named George Richardson from Lordstown, Ohio (approx. 35 miles from Independence, Ohio) discovered a wonderful award winning white hybrid hardy water lily known as *Gladstone* and William Tricker named it *Nymphaea Gladstoniana*. Today it is known as either *Gladstone* or *Gladstoniana*. During this period George Richardson also introduced a beautiful multi-petaled white hardy water lily and William Tricker named it *Nymphaea tuberosa Richardsonii* and is commonly known as *Richardsonii*.

Many of the hybrids of Marliac are still the favorites grown today. Hybridization is a little more difficult with the hardy water lilies than with the tropical water lilies and often takes years of meticulous breeding and attention. The historic literature over the years have described many different and beautiful hybrids.

NOTE: Some new hardy *"hybrids"* are being introduced today in the water lily industry. Careful consideration must be given to the *"assumed new"* seedlings found in ponds that occur by Mother Nature and are being introduced as new hybrids. Interestingly many hardy water lilies take on different characteristics with

Gladstone

different environmental concerns. For example, different soil conditions and environmental temperatures can emit different shades of color in the blooms. The size of the planting container or crowded growing conditions can have an effect on the size of the water lily bloom. If these concerns are not taken into consideration a new hardy water lily may be thought of as a different or new variety may be erroneous. It is best to appreciate a new hardy variety from an assumed seedling only if it has a distinct proven reproducible characteristic from the known existing or past historic named varieties of which there are many.

PLANTING INSTRUCTIONS. Hardy water lilies can be planted outside at the latitudes of Chicago, Cleveland and New York in the month of May. Southern states can plant earlier. The hardy water lilies can be planted anytime throughout the summer months.

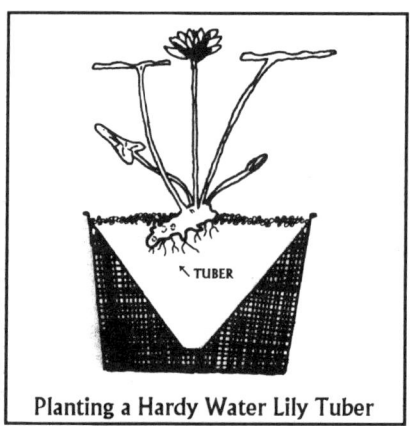

Planting a Hardy Water Lily Tuber

The growth of the hardy water lily is somewhat slower than the tropical water lily when transplanted. Within a few days after transplantation, many of the water lily pads may begin to die off. This is normal since the hardy tuber or root structure is beginning to grow new functioning immature roots and lily pads. Once the new immature water lily shoots emerge the root structure is becoming established and should not be disturbed.

Some hardy water lilies have a strong fibrous root system and would be planted similar to the tropical water lily. Other hardy water lilies have a fleshy rootstock, called a *"tuber"* and it is important that the tuber is planted with the growing point out of the soil and not buried. See pages 19 and 20, Steps 1-5 with illustrations.

CARE OF THE HARDY WATER LILY. Care of the hardy water lily is similar to that of the tropical water lily. However, since the hardy water lily is considered a perennial special precautions and care need to be done before and during winter.

Late in the season the hardy water lily will prepare for winter by developing a winter tuber in the soil. The flowers will stop being produced and the water lily pads will cease to grow. The main concern is to protect the developed hardy water lily tuber in the soil from freezing during winter. This can be done by placing the planting container with the hardy water lily at the bottom of the water garden pool.

If the water garden pool is shallow or may freeze solid, the planting container with tuber must be removed to a cold dark garden cellar. The water lily tuber in the planting container must be keep damp all winter.

In the spring, after the last freeze, the water lily planting container containing the tuber can now be returned to the original spot in the water garden. Mother Nature will now begin the growth process again for a new year as the sun warms the water and the rays of sunlight become more intense. As soon as a few new water lily pads are at the surface of the water the hardy water lily is ready for the fertilizer *Trico*™.

III. VICTORIA

The *Victoria* is an aquatic marvel from South America and named after Queen Victoria of England in 1849. This remarkable aquatic plant is easily recognized by its huge, round, floating leaves often six feet or more in diameter, with margins turned up at right angles to the water surface to a height of three to eight inches. The leaves resemble a large pizza pan. The flowers are nocturnal and are very large. On the day of opening the smell of pineapples is released into the atmosphere. The flowers last three days.

In 1893-94 William Tricker grew some seeds of the Victoria and noticed a different variety of plant, and later named it *Victoria trickeri*. The main characteristic of this variety is that it flowers much earlier in the summer than the other known existing Victorias and requires a lower temperature to grow.

Large water gardens are obviously necessary to grow the *Victoria*. The Victoria will take up at least a space of 400 square feet. However, planting in a

From William Tricker's 1897 text *The Water Garden*
Victoria trickeri

smaller container will restrict the growth spread and size and can be enjoyed in a smaller pond.

The *Victoria* does not have or make a tuber but is grown from seed each year. The plant is small when transplanted. It is planted in a good topsoil and fertilizer, *Praefecta™*. The larger the planting container the better. It is placed in the water garden with approximately two inches of water over the crown. As the plant begins to grow it can be lowered to a depth up to 24 inches above the crown. Floating leaves should not be submerged in the beginning growth. During the growing season 4 *Trico™* tablets a month should be added near the roots. Extreme care should be used since the stems and leaves have sharp spikes that can pierce the skin. Flowering in the Northern states should begin in July and continue to frost.

Water Lily Flowers make a Beautiful Table Arrangement Floating in a Bowl of Water.   Photograph by Robert V. Sawyer, William Tricker, Inc. circa 1930.

CHAPTER 3

LOTUS

The lotus is by far one of the most desired water garden plants for a water lily pool. The lotus creates a most striking sight in any pond. The round leaves, which can measure two to three feet across, are concave and shield-like and carried high above the water. The mystic flowers, which can reach 10 inches in size, and leaves are often on stems as high as five feet above the water. The dwarf varieties grow to about two feet high. A scoop of water in the hand and placed upon the round lotus leaves resembles mercury as it collects and rolls off the leaf, a most unusual sight.

Lotus

Patience is the key word in growing any lotus. The lotus are all hardy and once established will provide years of enjoyment from the foliage and flowers.

LOTUS FLOWERS. The flowers of the lotus have a very unusual mystic scent. Most varieties have huge flowers and are produced in shades of yellow, pink, red and white. The lotus flowers are "single" with a simple row of petals or "double" with multiple petals. The lotus will bloom for about three days and drop the petals. The lotus requires at least six hours of direct sunlight a day. Often the lotus needs a year to become established before blooming, however it is not uncommon to have blooms the very first year.

If the lotus flower is fertilized by insects a characteristic seed pod will develop. This lotus seed pod usually finds its way to our indoor vase and becomes a living fossil to remind us of our water garden during the winter months and the approaching new spring.

LOTUS GROWING CYCLE. Even though the lotus is hardy, it desires a great amount of heat during the growing season. Learning the growing cycle of the lotus helps understand the care and transplanting requirements.

The lotus winters as a tuber in the soil classically the shape of a banana. The size and shape of the tuber varies and can be just a few inches in length to as much as a foot or more long. At one end of the tuber is a delicate growing tip. As spring approaches the tuber sprouts from this growing tip. The sprout grows into a stem and an "underground runner". The underground runner will continue to grow through the soil and develop another growing tip and a new stem.

As the lotus begins growth, the stems will rise to the water's surface. At the surface a small round lotus leaf will begin to develop. Sometimes this leaf will float on the surface of the water as it prepares to become aerial and at other times the stem will emerge directly into the air before the round lotus leaf is revealed. Once the stems are aerial the leaves begin to grow to the varieties size.

Disturbing the roots of an established lotus plant can be harmful and cause its' death. Mature plants are not easily transplanted. This is why lotus tubers and special underground runners with immature leaves are used in starting new lotus plants.

PLANTING A LOTUS. As previously mentioned the lotus is obtained as a tuber or special underground runner.

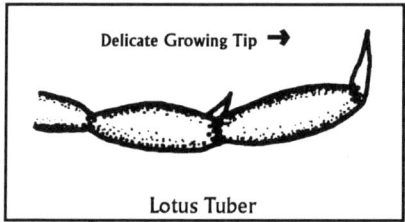
Lotus Tuber

The larger the container that the lotus is to be placed in the better the growth.

Fill a large container with good topsoil and mix one pound of *Praefecta*™ to three bushels of soil.

A. PLANTING A LOTUS TUBER:

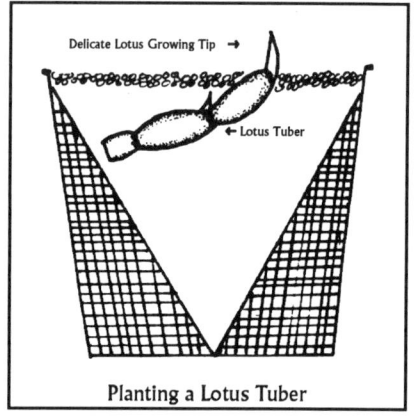
Planting a Lotus Tuber

Identify the growing tip on the lotus tuber. Be extremely careful NOT to touch or break the growing tip. If the lotus tuber was received in the mail, be extremely careful in opening the package since the growing tip may be hidden and can be broken when opening the package.

Hollow out a longitudinal area in the top of the soil. It is a good idea to make the top part of the soil wet with water to the consistency of a "soupy" mud. Carefully set the tuber into the hollowed out area and slowly push the mud around the lotus tuber. Do not break the growing tip. By using mud the prevention of packing dry soil and breaking the tip is avoided. The tip of the tuber should be slightly out of mud or above the soil level.

Cover the soil with approximately one to two inches of pea gravel allowing the growing tip to show out of the gravel. Be careful not to break the growing tip.

After the tuber is planted, gently lower the container into the water garden pool. The top of the container should be a few inches below the water level. After growth is seen the container can now be lowered to the recommended four to six inches below the water level.

B. PLANTING A LOTUS RUNNER. A lotus runner is developed later in the season after the tuber has sprouted. It often has a small stem and small round lotus leaf coming off the lotus runner. The runner will have the beginning of immature roots.

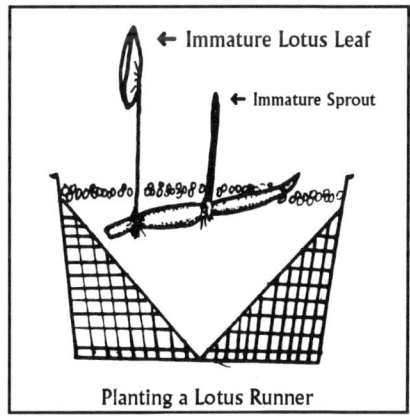

Planting a Lotus Runner

The lotus runner is planted similar to the tuber method by making a "soupy" mud mixture in the top layer of the planting container. The runner is placed in this soupy mud mixture and slowly pressed into position and covered with the pea gravel. The small stem with leaf should be above the pea gravel and not buried. Slowly place the planted container into the water garden allowing only a few inches of water above the container. Any leaves on the runner should not be below the water level. Once growth commences the container can be lowered into the water garden to the recommended depth of four to six inches.

CARE OF THE LOTUS. Once the lotus begins growth, the plant should not be disturbed. At times a small growth occurs the first season only to be followed by a spectacular growing season the second year. The lotus loves intense sunlight and if given a large enough container of topsoil and fertilizer will produce a wonderful plant. Once growth commences every month a *Trico*™ fertilizer tablet should be used.

At the end of summer the lotus will begin to go dormant. This can be identified when the flowers are no longer produced and the round lotus leaves will begin to turn brown and die. Protection of the tubers from freezing in the planting container is essential. This can be done by lowering the container to the bottom of the water garden insuring that this area will not freeze during winter.

In the spring, after the last freeze, the container with the wintered lotus can be raised to a few inches from the water surface. Nature will now sprout the wintered lotus and the enchantment returns.

A Lotus Pond
From the 1897 book *The Water Garden* by William Tricker.

CHAPTER 4

SHALLOW WATER AND BOG PLANTS

Natural ponds have a profusion of flags, rushes, reeds and small flowering plants which delight the eye. Water garden pools will be more attractive and much more naturalistic when planted with clumps of these ornamental and semi-tropical plants.

Planting of Shallow Water and Bog Plants. Shallow water and bog plants are easily planted in good topsoil with a mixture of a fertilizer known as *Praefecta*™. *Praefecta*™ is used as one pound per three bushels of soil.

Different size of potting containers can be used for single or multiple plantings. As with most plants the size of the planting container will determine the growth size of the plant. Once the planting container is selected, hollow out a small depression in the soil and gently place the roots into the depression. Carefully pack soil around the roots in this depression and cover the soil with an approximate 1/2 inch of pea gravel. The potted aquatic plant is placed into the water garden on a shelf or supported underneath with a cover of water over the crown from two to six inches. Since plants are at different sizes when planting make sure that the plant is never totally submerged when placing into the water garden. As the plant grows it can be adjusted to the correct depth. Additional planting techniques will be discussed with some varieties listed.

I. HARDY PLANTS.

The following hardy aquatic plants are planted with approximately two inches of water over the top of the soil.

ARROWHEAD (*Sagittaria* species). The group of *arrowheads* are named for the shape of the foliage which resembles an Indian arrowhead. Old literature commonly refers to the plant more appropriately as "Arrow-leaf". Another common name is "Duck Potato" derived from the round edible tuber formed in the winter that ducks find appetizing. Depending upon the variety, the arrowheads can be found to have single or double white flowers. The arrowheads stand one to three feet above the water.

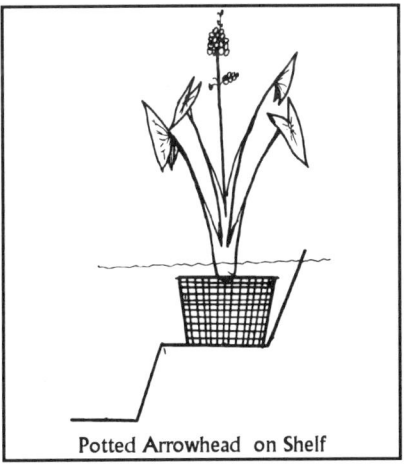
Potted Arrowhead on Shelf

They transplant exceptionally well and grow rapidly. In spring, the arrowheads often begin growth later than the other aquatic plants.

HARDY CALLA (*Calla palustris*). (WATER ARUM, MARSH CALLA). Hardy calla is a very attractive plant that bears many heart-shaped leaves and a small white arum-like flower that blooms May through June. This is followed in autumn by a globular cluster of red berries. It grows by rootstocks. The plant is of interest as one of the few known to be fertilized by snails. The height of the

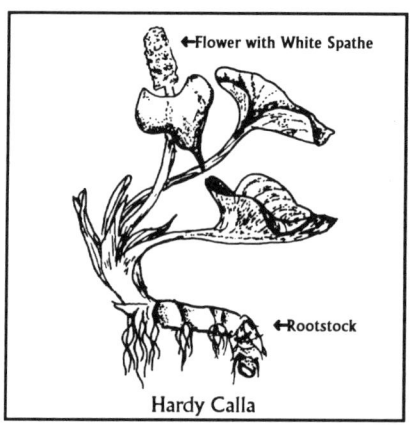
Hardy Calla

plant is approximately six inches to a foot. The plant grows exceptionally well in the spring and develops wonderfully unusual and attractive flowers. Plant the rootstock directly into the soil. Make sure that the leaves are out of the water when placing the potted hardy calla into the water garden.

CARDINAL FLOWER. (*Lobelia cardinalis*). Cardinal flower is an attractive plant with extremely fiery red flowers that attract hummingbirds. It is often planted in a location in the water garden so that the deep red flowers are mirrored in the depths of the water garden pool. The cardinal flower will reach a height of two to four feet and flower from July to September. The cardinal flower needs only wet feet. Never submerge the entire plant with leaves under the water. As growth begins, lower to the final water depth of two inches. The flowers should make seeds in the fall and the rootstock will bring new growth in the spring.

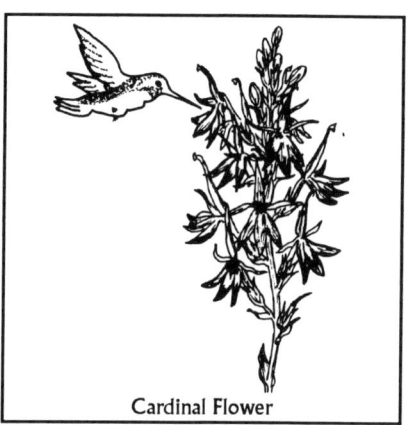
Cardinal Flower

WATER PLANTAIN. (*Alisma* species). The water plantains are similar to the arrowheads but do not have leaves with lobes. The leaves are broad and coarsely veined. Pinkish or white flowers are at the ends of stiff stems rising high above the leaves. The broad towering spires become hard and woody after flowering and persist throughout the winter, catching the snow on their outspread arms making a most beautiful winter sight. The plant grows from two to three feet high.

PURPLE LOOSESTRIFE (*Lythrum salicaria*, variety Morden's Pink). This variety of purple loosestrife is a showy plant that has a native relative who has become a nuisance in certain areas of the United States. This variety is sterile, but fortunately still attracts a multitude of butterflies, bumble bees and the hummingbird moth. The reddish-purple blooms will grow to a height of three to four feet.

BLUE IRIS (*Iris versicolor*) or **YELLOW IRIS** (*Iris pseudacorus*). The blue and yellow iris are often a common sight along a natural pond. The leaves are flat and sword-like. The plant height is from two to four feet, the blue iris being somewhat smaller. The flowers are produced in the spring and will last a few weeks. Seeds are often produced, however the rootstock will produce a new plant in the spring.

FLOWERING RUSH (*Botomus umbellatus*). Flowering rush is a beautiful aquatic that produces spreading umbels of dainty rose-pink flowers on stout erect flower stems. The leaves are broad, sheathed at the base, triangular in cross section and at the top are pointed in a sword-like shape. The plant reaches from one to three feet high and flowers July through August. See illustration on page 38.

WATERCRESS (*Nasturtium officinale*). The watercress has dark green leaves and small white flowers and can form a pleasing contrast to the more feathery submerged oxygenating plants. It will often grow into a beautiful tangled mass.

Iris

Watercress

HORSETAIL (*Equisetum hyemale*) (SCOURING RUSH). The horsetail resembles bamboo in the water garden pool. Also known as "scouring rush" because sections of this unique plant were bound into small bundles that were used by pioneer families for "scouring" floors, tables, etc. It has a hollow stem that is jointed with no true leaves but a toothed sheath at each joint and grows one to two feet high.

COMMON SWEET FLAG (*Acorous calamus*) or **DWARF SWEET FLAG** (*Acorous gramineus*). The leaf blades of the sweet flags are similar to the iris. When any part of the plant is cut or bruised a spicy sweet citrus scent is released. The **common sweet flag** will reach heights of two to four feet and the **dwarf sweet flag** will reach heights of up to a foot. They make an unusual flower.

WILD RICE (*Zizania aquatica*). Wild rice is a very desirable aquatic grass, being one of the most attractive plants for decoration in the water garden pool. Once the plant produces seeds it becomes a most spectacular sight as the seeds dangle from the stems as high as nine feet. Flowers with seeds are visible in July through August.

LIZARD'S TAIL (*Saururus cernuus*). The small fragrant flowers of Lizard's tail that are produced at the end of the plant resemble a "lizard's tail", thus alluding to name. The leaves are heart shaped. The plant grows to a height of two feet.

FORGET-ME-NOT (*Myosotis scorpiodes*). This species is the "water" forget-me-not that will bloom early summer and continue throughout the growing season with sky blue flowers. It can grow from six to ten inches in height.

Forget-Me-Not

MARSH MARIGOLD (*Caltha palustris*). The Marsh marigold is a beautiful native plant which is almost the earliest to flower in the water garden. Marsh marigold produces beautiful rich golden yellow flowers in wild profusion. The flowers resemble gigantic buttercups. It will grow from nine to 15 inches high. As spring slowly progresses into summer the Marsh marigold will cease to flower and growth will diminish. The rootstock will provide a new plant the following spring.

GRACEFUL CAT-TAIL (*Typha laxmannii*). The graceful cat-tail possesses an air of grace and dignity not encountered by any other group of hardy aquatics. It is a slender plant two to four feet tall with very narrow leaves easily moved by the slightest breathe of wind.

The following plants should be planted in six inches of water:

WATER HAWTHORNE (*Aponogeton disachyus*). Water hawthorne is a most admirable plant that is known for its long blooming characteristics. It has dark green strap-like leaves about a foot long often mottled with brown or purple blotches. The beautiful white flowers with contrasting coal black stamens make this one of the loveliest of all water plants. The flowers emit a strong fragrance resembling a wild hawthorne, hence the name. The plant will begin to flower and grow rapidly in the spring when the water is cool. During the summer, in intense heat, the water hawthorne will begin a dormancy period only to return when the water cools. It will often continue to grow and bloom well into the fall especially when the water becomes cooler.

CAT-TAILS (*Typha* species). A true mark to any water garden is the cat-tail which can be identified by most. A small breeze will add a graceful movement to any water garden. The **common cat-tail** (*Typha latifolia*) is one of the native swamp plants. The common cat-tail will reach a height of eight feet in large planting containers. The **dwarf catkin cat-tail** (*Typha gracilis*) grows from three to four feet tall with light brown, almost egg-shaped catkins. The **variegated cat-tail** (*Typha latifolia variegata*) adds a different "cat-tail" look to the water garden. It is distinctly striped with light green and white leaves and grows four to five feet tall.

BOGBEAN (*Menyanthes trifoliata*). Bogbean is a wonderful marginal cover that grows by a creeping rootstock. The fragrant white flowers are borne in the spring on stout stalks that are fringed and suffused with pink.

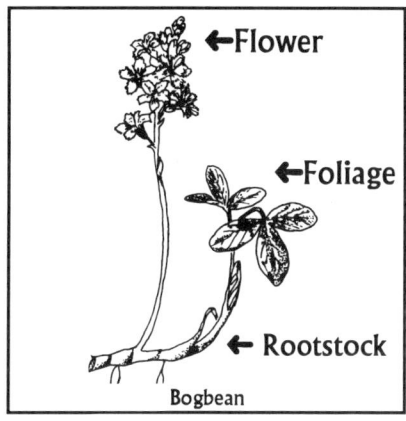
Bogbean

FLOATING HEART (*Nymphoides peltata*). Floating heart provides a wonderful display of delicate yellow fringed buttercup-like flowers among the handsome green and brown mottled foliage reminiscent of a pygmy water lily. It grows rapidly and flowers very freely.

ARROW ARUM (*Peltandra virginica*). Arrow arum is a handsome plant that produces glossy, arrow-shaped leaves that are very fleshy with a white arum flower.

It will usually grow to from 12 to 18 inches tall and can grow very large in natural ponds.

HARDY THALIA (*Thalia dealbata*). Hardy thalia has tall grayish leaves and grows from three to five feet tall. The small reddish-purple flowers are held high on stems. The plant is dusted over with a minute white powder which gives a pretty frosted appearance.

PICKEREL RUSH (*Pontederia cordata*). Pickerel rush is considered by many to be the finest blue-flowered hardy aquatic in cultivation. It is a strong growing plant that attains a height of one to two feet. The leaves are smooth, shining olive-green.

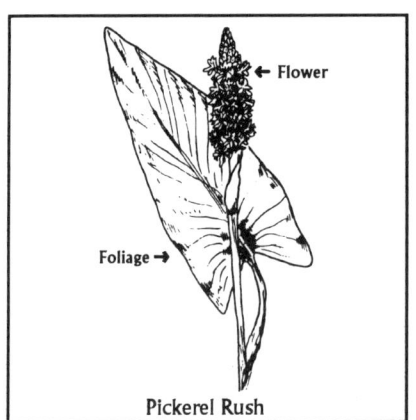

Pickerel Rush

VARIEGATED FOUR LEAF WATER CLOVER (*Marsilea multica*). This Four Leaf Water Clover is an aquatic plant that has lightly variegated leaves which float quietly on the water surface. If allowed to grow near the edge of the water garden the water clover will send up aerial leaves.

WATER PENNYWORT (*Hydrocotyle verticillata*). Water Pennywort has round penny-like leaves that stand four to six inches above the water. The plant grows fast by the means of runners and is very showy. See illustration on page 38.

PARROT FEATHER (*Myriophyllum proserpinacoides*). Parrot feather is a favorite plant for the fountain basin or growing at the edges of the water garden. The leaves are a delicate whitish-green and grow in a dense feathery whorl around the stem. [Planting Note: If there are no roots on the stems of the parrot feather, plant the stems into the soil and allow the feathery leaves to be above the water level when placing into the water garden. Roots will then develop.]

II. TROPICAL PLANTS:

The following tropical aquatic plants are planted with approximately two inches of water over the crown of the plant.

PAPYRUS (*Cyperus* species). The papyrus adds a beautiful effect to the water garden. The papyrus have a tuft of long thread-like leaves at the top of the plant and gives the water garden a novel appearance. **Dwarf Papyrus** (*Cyperus haspan var. vivparus*) grows to about two feet. **Papyrus** (*Cyperus papyrus*) is the famous Egyptian paper plant and can grow five to eight feet tall.

CHINESE WATER CHESTNUT (*Eleocharis tuberosa*). The Chinese water chestnut is a very attractive plant with cylindrical stems. It produces a tuber that is used in oriental cooking, hence its name.

NEW PICKEREL RUSH (*Pontederia paniculata*). The new pickerel rush has heart-shaped leaves that are very dark green and shiny. It is taller than the hardy pickerel rush. The flowers are borne freely and are produced continually throughout the flowering season. The flowers resemble our hardy pickerel rush except that there are two shades of color in the petals, light and dark violet blue. Being a tropical plant it grows rapidly providing a continued season of wonderful blooms.

PRIMROSE WILLOW (*Jussiaea longifolia*). The primrose willow is an erect plant two to three feet high with attractive narrow foliage and bright yellow blossoms.

SPIDER LILY (*Hymenocallis caribaea*). The spider lily produces clusters of unusual fragrant white flowers. The petals are narrow and curving giving the plant a characteristic spider-like appearance.

SPIRAL PALM. The spiral palm resembles an umbrella palm but only grows to about a foot tall. The attractive leaves spiral around the base of the plant.

TEMPLE PLANT (*Hygrophila corymbosa*). The temple plant is covered with fine hairs and is brownish green to reddish green with beautiful blue flowers.

UMBRELLA PALM (*Cyperus alternifolius*). The umbrella palm has "umbrella" heads of foliage and numerous flat, pale-brown spikelets of flowers. It can be easily moved indoors and used as a house plant in the winter months.

Umbrella Palm

DWARF UMBRELLA PALM (*Cyperus alternifolius var gracilis*). The dwarf umbrella palm is smaller and more slender than the umbrella palm and grows to a height of 18 inches.

VELVET LEAF (*Limnocharis flava*). The velvet leaf is a member of the orchid family having sunrise yellow flowers edged in white. After blooming the flowering stems will slowly drop into the water and produce a new plant. The leaves are oval and have a pastel green color.

The following tropical aquatic plants are planted with six inches of water over the crown of the plant:

FOUR LEAF WATER CLOVER (*Marsilia drummundi*). Leaves resemble the lawn four leaf clover and form a mosiac pattern on the surface. In crowded spots it sends up a luxurious growth of aerial leaves. See illustration on page 38.

TROPICAL THALIA (*Thalia divaricata*). The tropical thalia is a larger and stouter plant than the hardy thalia. It will grow five to 10 feet high with zigzag spikes of purple flowers.

PURPLE WATER HYACINTH (*Eichornia azurea*). Purple water hyacinth is a creeping plant without the floating bulbs of the ordinary floating water hyacinth. Makes attractive purple flowers.

WATER POPPY (*Hydrocleys nymphoides*). The water poppy is a beautiful aquatic with thick, oval floating, deep green leaves and handsome three petaled flowers resembling a poppy. The flowers are light yellow and stand well above the water and last for a day. The plant is very free-flowering and most prolific.

WATER SENSITIVITY PLANT (*Neptunia oleracea*). The water sensitivity plant will close its' leaves when touched. The plant has a floatation system of bulbous material that allows it to spread across the pond. It produces a yellow flower that is held above the leaves.

Water Sensitivity Plant

MELLON SWORDS (*Echinodorus osiris*). The mellon swords are one of the most beautiful species of this genus. It can be grown in a bright or slightly shady area of the water garden. The young leaves are intensive red in color and fades as the leaves become larger to a dark green. The white flowers bloom above the water and the plant can grow to three feet tall.

SNOWFLAKES (*Nymphoides* species). The snowflakes are charming plants that add beauty to all water gardens. The leaves are heart-shaped and float on the water surface and produce wonderful fringed delicate flowers. The **Water Snowflake** (*Nymphoides indica*) is a delicate small plant and has small clusters of dainty white flowers with yellow centers. The **Giant Water Snowflake** (*Nymphoides*

Water Poppy

species) has leaves up to four inches across and produces the largest flowers of the snowflakes. The **Variegated Water Snowflake** (*Nymphoides indicum varigata*) has beautiful green and bronze variegated leaves. The **New Zealand Water Snowflake** (*Nymphoides* species) is similar to the water snowflake but has a purple edging around the leaves.

PRIMROSE CREEPER (*Jussiaea repens*). Primrose creeper is a rapid growing plant with "creeping" or floating stems. It has waxy green leaves and a profusion of inch wide bright, golden yellow flowers standing above the water. The plant thrives well in both sunlight or shade.

BUTTERFLY LILY (*Hedychium coronarium*). The butterfly lily is a tall canna-like plant with large leaves and very fragrant white blossoms borne in umbels. The flowers can be found in salmon, white, apricot, red or yellow.

RADICANS (*Echinodorus cordifolius*). The radicans have pale green leaves with white flowers. The plant can grow to three feet high.

III. MISCELLANEOUS SHALLOW WATER PLANTS:

TAROS (*Colocasia* species). The taros contain a tuberous plant grown chiefly for their foliage. They are planted in shallow water or at a depth to keep the soil moist. All taros are easy to grow. They make an attractive display at the edges of the water garden or as a centerpiece. In the winter

Green Taro

the taros can be brought indoors and used as a house plant until spring.

a. **Red Stem Taro** has unique foliage in rich green or dark purplish-red stems. It is a strong grower.

b. **Dwarf Green Taro** has shiny leaves on bluish green stems.

c. **Ruby Taro** is the only taro with a distinct red stem and violet leaves. It grows three to five feet tall.

d. **Imperial Taro** is the finest of the Asiatic taros. The leaves are attractively blotched a dark brown and violet back.

e. **Violet Stem Taro** is one of the most beautiful of the taros. The leaves are a beautiful blue-green. The stems, midribs and veins underneath the leaves are a lovely lavender, the same color repeated in the edges of the leaves.

f. **Green Taro** is the most beautiful form of taro with large green leaves. The green taro grows to about three feet and fills out the sides. It makes a full centerpiece focal point or a nice back drop for water lilies. It is a very good growing plant.

g. **Jade Taro** has unusual bright green shiny leaves and grows to about three feet high. The flowers are clustered on a yellow spike-like stalk, at the base of an open variegated green and white spathe which is very attractive.

ASTILBE (*Plumy spirea*). Astilbes are also known as the *Feather Flower* and is one of the most beautiful perennial that can grow in the shade. Lovely feathery clusters of flower spikes are found in shades of red, pink and white. Stems grow to about two feet and the flowers bloom in June and July. The astilbe has elegant dark red-green to light green glossy foliage. It is best to plant the astilbe in soil that is kept moist next to the water garden or if placed into the water garden making sure that the potted plant is at a height that only the soil keeps wet.

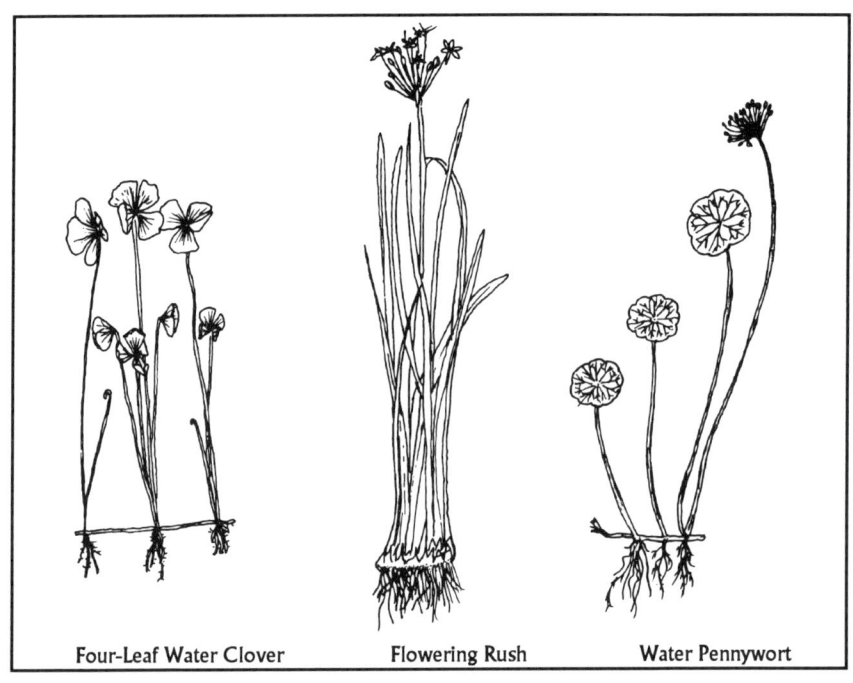

Four-Leaf Water Clover   Flowering Rush   Water Pennywort

CHAPTER 5

FLOATING and OXYGENATING PLANTS

I. FLOATING PLANTS:

Some of the finest aquatics will grow and bloom merely floating on the water surface, deriving nourishment from the air and water. They add a very unusual and attractive feature to any water garden. A certain amount of floating vegetation is of value to the water garden pool. It provides shelter and shade for the fish and by excluding the sunlight it will deter rapid multiplication of undesirable algae. Many floating plants provide an excellent spawning medium for fish.

AZOLLA (*Azolla caroliniana*). Azolla is also known as "water fern" or "fairy moss". It is a small free flowering fern made up of lobes of blue-green velvet leaves (fronds) with rootlets on the undersides. In the autumn Azolla commonly turns a rust red. They increase rapidly by dividing in the summer and die down completely in the winter. Spores are produced but a harsh cold winter can kill the spores.

DUCKWEED (*Lemna minor*). Duckweed a favorite food of fish. The duckweed will commonly reproduce by dividing as it grows across the water surface. They have small roots hanging under the body of the leaf. It is hardy.

SALVINIA (*Salvinia rotundifolia*). Salvinia is a fern with stiff hairs on the upper heart-shaped leaf and hanging roots on the underside. The leaves appear as bits of velvet connected by a thread. The roots are commonly fed upon by fish. It is not hardy.

WATER HYACINTH (*Eichhornia crassipes major*). The water hyacinth has pale purple flowers with a central yellow spot and shiny dark green leaves. The stems are expanded into bulbs which serve as air chambers and allows the plant to float. Propagation occurs rapidly by means of runners at the surface of the water. The long bushy roots are excellent for receiving the spawn of fish. The water hyacinth will flower more frequently if the roots touch soil. It is an excellent plant that can be used to reduce algal blooms. The plant needs plenty of warmth and as autumn approaches will die completely in cold weather where snow is eminent. It is not hardy.

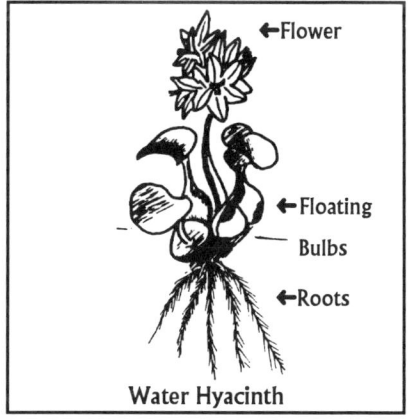

Water Hyacinth

WATER LETTUCE (*Pistia stratoides*). *Water lettuce* or *Shell Flower* is an interesting floating plant with shell-like rosettes of pulpy and hairy leaves that are spirally arranged around the axis. The long feathery rootlets dangle in the water and provide a good spawning medium for fish. The water lettuce will grow in full sun or the shade. It needs plenty of warmth and as autumn approaches will die completely in cold weather where snow is eminent in the winter. It is not hardy.

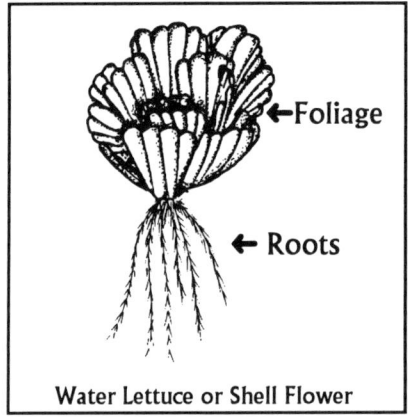

Water Lettuce or Shell Flower

FLOATING FERN (*Ceratopteris pteridoides*). The floating fern will float on top of the water and make a beautiful dense mass of rosette pea-green leaves, at times a foot or more in diameter. Often the plants are about six inches in diameter and are very pleasing in appearance. The leaves have a wavy margin and are egg shaped or triangular. The plants are easily propagated because they form many plantlets on the edges of the leaves. The feathery roots hang down into the water and provide a spawning medium for fish and a place for the small fry to hide. It grows good in partial shade to full sun. It is not hardy.

HOW TO PLANT FLOATING PLANTS: Floating plants are simply placed directly upon the surface of water.

II. OXYGENATING PLANTS:

Every pool needs oxygenating plants to keep the water crystal clear and pure. These plants grow under the water just like the plants seen growing naturally in ponds and lakes. Carbon dioxide is a natural product produced from respiration of animals and plants in the water garden. The oxygenating plants, using sunlight during the day, absorb this carbon dioxide and liberate pure oxygen into the water. This oxygen can be used by the abundant life in the pond keeping the water pure.

LUDWIGIA (*Ludwigia* species). Ludwigia is a good grower at the edges of the water garden and desired for its very decorative appearance. The undersides often become a beautiful red color in intense light.

HYGROPHILIA (*Hygrophilia* sp). Pronounced "high-grof'i-la" and grows rapidly in direct sunlight. **Red Hygrophilia** has a beautiful red color mixed with dark green of the foliage. **Green Hygrophilia** has light green foliage.

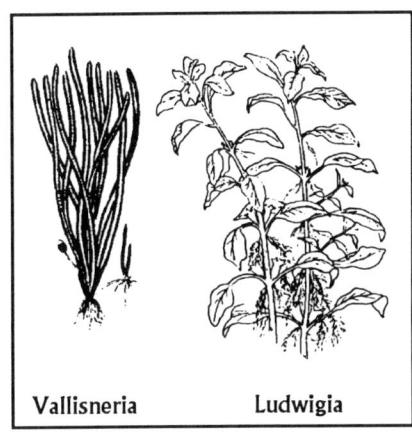

Vallisneria   Ludwigia

VALLISNERIA (*Vallisneria* sp.). Vallisneria is a grass-like plant that is an excellent oxygenator. Vallisneria grows and multiplies constantly by runners. These runners naturally root themselves into a new plant. **Vallisneria Spirilis** is much smaller than **Vallisneria Gigantea (Jungle Vallisneria)**. It is a very attractive aquatic plant.

ANACHARIS (*Elodea canadensis*). Anacharis is one of the most commonly used water garden oxygenators. It has a rapid growth and produces an abundant amount of oxygen in good sunlight. The plant provides an excellent dense mass for fish to spawn or protection for the fry. They produce small tiny floating white flowers on trailing thread-like stalks.

WATER MILFOIL (*Myriophyllum* sp). Milfoils are very decorative. They are delicate in appearance with a green tangle of fine linear leaf segments. They are very suitable for fish and fry because they carry a multitude of numerous plankton. Plankton are microscopic plant life that is an excellent food source. They also provide an excellent spawning medium for the fish.

MONEYWORT (*Lysimachia nummularia*). Moneywort is also known as Creeping Jenny or Mouse Ear. It gives a carpeting effect at the water side. The small round leaves grow in opposite pairs. Bright golden cup-shaped flowers appear during the early summer months and have a scent similar to peaches. It is hardy.

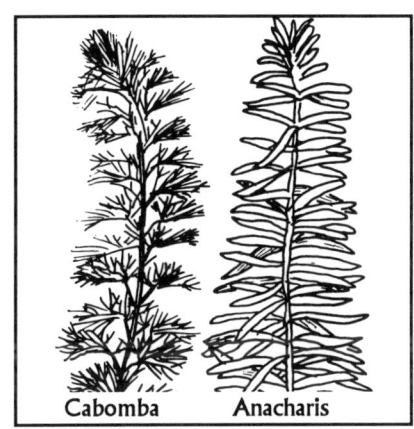

Cabomba   Anacharis

CABOMBA (*Cabomba caroliniana*). Cabomba or Fanwort is a great oxygenator. Cabomba has fan-like, bright green leaves that are displayed beautifully in water.

SAGITTARIA (*Sagittaria* sp). The variety of sagittaria that is considered an oxygenator makes a wonderful rosette-like dark green plant which propagates by the means of runners. It is propagated by runners and is hardy.

HOW TO PLANT OXYGENATORS:

When received, if the oxygenators have rubber bands holding them together, remove the rubber bands. Using a suitable sized planting container with a good topsoil mixed with *Praefecta*™, hollow out a hole. Place the roots or stems into this hole and gently pack the soil around them. Cover the soil with a layer of pea gravel. Place the planted container into the water garden totally submerging the oxygenator. The water over the top of the oxygenator can vary from just a few inches to a few feet. As long as sunlight reaches through the water to the oxygenator, it will grow. Fertilize with *Trico*™ every month. Growth will begin and will add color and movement in the depths of the water garden.

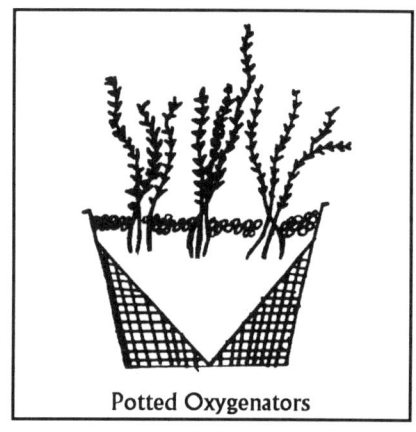
Potted Oxygenators

CHAPTER 6

Fish add a beauty to the water garden pool. They combine color, movement and a grace that cannot be added with any other type of gardening. If nature had its way it would definitely put fish into every water garden.

I. WATER QUALITY.

Before introducing fish for a water garden pool some basic understanding of water quality is necessary. This involves the terms **pH, nitrogen cycle, ammonia, nitrates** and **nitrites**.

pH. In 1927, history was made when a chemical engineer by the name of Mr. William G. O'Brien, vice-president and secretary of William Tricker, Inc., Independence, Ohio realized that pH and fish health were related. This led to his introduction of the first *pH test kit* for aquatic life. Decades of evidence found that Mr. W.G. O'Brien was correct with his concern for the pH of the water correlating with fish health. Today, testing the pH for water quality is routine and is performed around the world in aquariums and water garden pools.

The pH of the water garden pool is one of the most important and simple tests that can be made. The term pH stands for "potential hydrogen" concentration. The

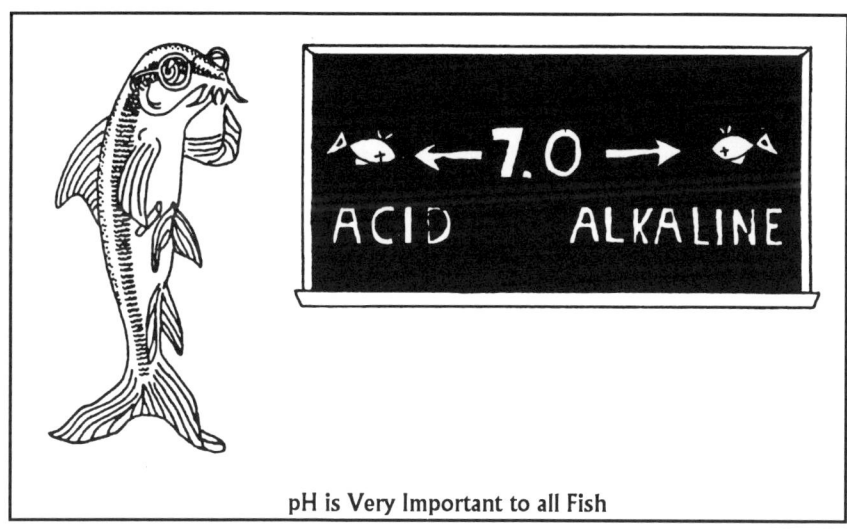

pH is Very Important to all Fish

pH is the measure of the quantity of acid or charged hydrogen ions (H+) in the water. The pH scale is from 0 to 14. The number seven represents a neutral reading. Any pH number lower than seven is increasingly acid and any number greater than seven is increasingly alkaline.

Most species of fish live in a pH range from a pH six to a pH eight. As the pH number drops from pH six (becoming acid, a condition known as *acidosis*), fish react by gasping for air and attempting to jump out of the water. As the pH number rises from pH eight (becoming alkaline, known as *alkalinosis*), fish begin to show frayed fins, skin discoloration and gill irritation.

A pH test kit contains a method of determining the numerical pH. Periodic checking the pH of the water garden pool will prevent a disastrous surprise of finding a fish kill with a deadly pH. It will also help understand the occurrence of any diseases acquired by the fish or give an ecological clue to the water garden pool's health.

If the pH of the water garden pool is not within the correct range of pH 6 to pH 8 then chemicals can be added to bring the pH into range. Using chemicals to adjust the pH should be a temporary situation. It is very important to try to find why the pH is not in the correct range and correct that situation without chemicals. The pH should not be changed more than 0.1 to 0.2 units per day.

NITROGEN CYCLE. One of the best ways to kill fish is to upset the *"nitrogen cycle"* of the water garden pool. A basic understanding of this important cycle is crucial. The name is derived from the element **"nitrogen"** as it is **"cycled"** into different chemical compounds which effect the water quality and fish health. During this cycle the nitrogen chemical compounds become toxic at different stages. If the nitrogen cycle is upset or disrupted these nitrogen chemicals can accumulate in toxic levels and cause diseases in fish which may lead to death or directly cause fish kills. Thus, the nitrogen cycle must continue without disturbance in the water garden pool.

Carefully study the diagram titled "The Nitrogen Cycle." on the next page. To understand the nitrogen cycle, begin with the fish at the top of the diagram. Other aquatic animal life, such as snails, frogs, clams, salamanders etc., could also be substituted for the fish. The animal life in the water garden will produce wastes. In addition, uneaten fish food, decaying animals and decaying plants are depicted at the beginning of this cycle. These all produce a nitrogen chemical known as **AMMONIA**, which subsequently has a portion known as **TOXIC AMMONIA** which can be deadly to fish at high concentrations.

AMMONIA. Ammonia increases can destroy the protective mucus membranes and gills of the fish and cause internal bleeding. The fish will show rapid and

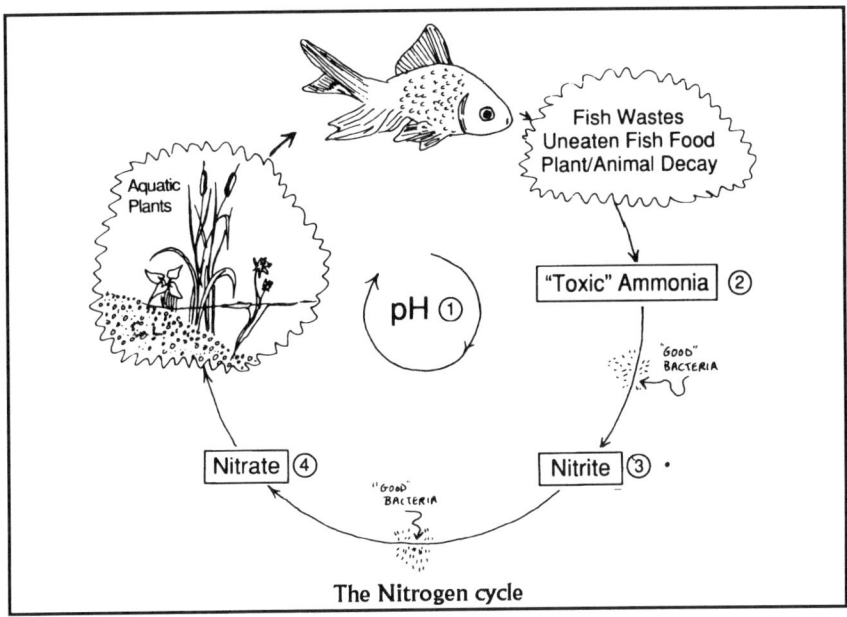
The Nitrogen cycle

irregular swimming and gasping for air at the surface. This observation is often mistaken as a lack of oxygen in the water but is related to the destruction or inability of red blood cells to carry oxygen caused by the presence of increased ammonia.

If the ammonia levels increase, the fish cannot breathe due to the lack or ability of red blood cells to carry the life sustaining oxygen, not the lack of oxygen in the water.

Ammonia exists in two forms depending upon the pH or temperature of the water, "**regular ammonia**" and "**toxic ammonia**". An increase in toxic ammonia can be deadly to fish. At a pH of eight, 5% of the ammonia is toxic and at a pH of nine, 30% of the ammonia is toxic. In addition, as the temperature of the water increases the ammonia becomes more toxic. Thus, as the pH and temperature of the water rises the amount of toxic ammonia increases and can become deadly to fish.

The next step after ammonia is produced is the proliferation of a specific bacteria. These specific bacteria (scientifically called *Nitrosomonas*) uses oxygen in their metabolism and are considered "good bacteria" in the water garden pool. A type of non-oxygenating bacteria that can live without oxygen are not desirable in the water garden environment. It is the non-oxygenating bacteria that gives the rotten egg smell to stagnant or polluted water that is characteristically low in oxygen. The reason the "good bacteria" are desirable is because they continue the nitrogen cycle by having the ability in the presence of oxygen to break down or remove the ammonia produced into the next nitrogen chemical, **NITRITE**. The non-oxygenating bacteria do not have this ability.

After the nitrite is produced another specific bacteria (*Nitrobacter*), again one that thrives with oxygen and is a "good bacteria", breaks down the nitrite in the presence of oxygen into another nitrogen chemical, **NITRATE**. It is the nitrates produced that can be used by the aquatic plants or algae as a source of food.

The nitrogen cycle has made a complete cycle when fish or other animals in the water garden feed on the aquatic plants or algae that are using the nitrates as food. Once this occurs the cycle repeats and the water garden is considered ecologically balanced and no toxic chemicals are accumulated.

TESTING FOR AMMONIA, NITRITES AND NITRATES.

An upset in the nitrogen cycle will cause an increase in one of the nitrogen chemicals produced: ammonia, nitrites or nitrates.

For example, if the good bacteria were not present or destroyed, the ammonia would become increased. Some pesticides or prescribed fish medication can kill the "good bacteria". The good bacteria are found in nature on aquatic plants or in the water garden soil and are highly desirable in maintaining the important nitrogen cycle.

Another example of an upset of the cycle is over feeding fish and it has been said that "*many kill their fish through kindness-they feed them too often*". Uneaten fish food will begin to decay and increase the ammonia concentration in the water garden.

The temperature of the water is important in feeding fish. The colder the temperature the less the food the fish will eat due to the diminished activity of the fish. When the temperatures are around 40 degrees Fahrenheit the fish usually will not feed. Since their metabolism is slowed by the cold water temperature the fish require little or no energy food source.

Ammonia, nitrate and nitrite testing are easy and simple tests that can be performed along side the water garden pool. Increases can indicate an upset in the nitrogen cycle.

II. BIOLOGICAL FILTER SYSTEMS.

To ensure that the nitrogen cycle continues, a biological filter may be used. For example, if ammonia has become a

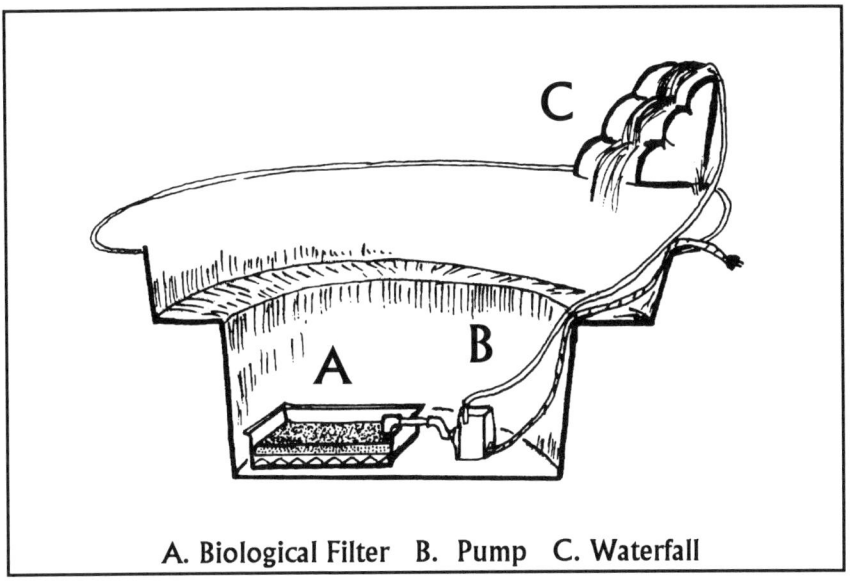

A. Biological Filter B. Pump C. Waterfall

persistent problem a biological filter can reduce the ammonia. A biological filter is an artificial system to insure that the nitrogen cycle continues with the "good bacteria". It actually provides a medium or environment for the "good bacteria" to live. A water pump will pass water through a filter that allows the "good bacteria" to thrive on the ammonia and nitrites. These bacteria will convert the ammonia into nitrates and keep the nitrogen cycle functioning properly.

A waterfall connected in conjunction with the biological filter system is a good idea. This will add oxygen into the water for the "good bacteria" as well as the other animals such as the fish.

III. FISH FEEDING.

Since the fish are in an "artificial" environment in a water garden pool they will need a good food source to stay healthy. A variety of fish foods is recommended. There are two such sources available: live foods and prepared foods. Both should be used if possible to keep the fish healthy.

1. **Live Fish Foods**: Live foods are often considered the best food source for any fish. Often live foods are more difficult to supply, but a true effort to obtain live foods is rewarded by healthy fish.

Feed Fish a Variety of Foods

DAPHNIA. One of the best live foods for fish is a small pin-head crustacean known as "Daphnia". They are consumed by fish in a greedy manner, showing their desire and excitable attitude for this food. In the early spring daphnia are abundant and often can be specially requested from a reputable supplier.

MOSQUITO LARVAE. Mosquito larvae are a real treat for fish and Nature provides this food. They are not seen in the water garden due to the strong appetite by the fish for this larvae. In fact, if a water garden is plagued with mosquitoes a remedy is to add fish. The fish will quickly devour any mosquito larvae. Mosquito larvae can be found in small pockets of standing water and a cupful added to your water garden will delight any fish.

DUCKWEED. Duckweed, an aquatic floating plant, is an excellent food for fish. This can be considered a vegetable for the fish and they truly enjoy it. To insure a good supply, place some duckweed in a tub of water kept in sunlight. Remove portions of duckweed from this tub periodically and feed the fish.

2. Prepared Fish Foods. When using prepared fish foods often a different variety is selected to insure all the necessary nutrients.

Floating foods can be used to train the fish to come to the surface of the water to feed. This is a very exciting and fascinating site. However, a clever raccoon can approach the water garden, swish his paw in the water and the trained fish will approach the surface only to find a hungry raccoon. In this circumstance, where raccoons are a problem, only sinking fish foods should be used.

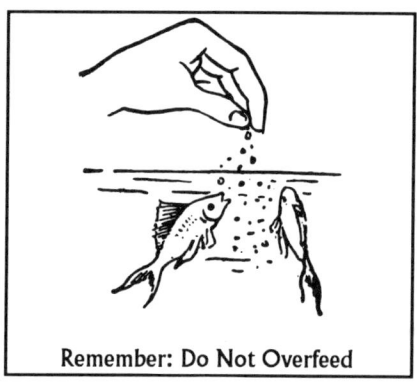

Remember: Do Not Overfeed

One of the hardest things to do is not to overfeed the fish. It is best to sprinkle a small amount of food in the water.

Wait for the fish to eat the food. If they eat the food sprinkle another small amount. If in five minutes the food remains, do not feed any more food. Fish love to dart around and enjoy movement in your pond and sometimes are thought to be eating. Any unconsumed food will be an environment for fungus and bacterial decay and increase the ammonia levels. It is best to learn the feeding habits of your fish.

Fish eat less when the temperature of the water is cooler. As winter approaches the aquatic plants will go dormant and the fish will begin a resting period. This resting period will continue until spring and the fish should not be fed. Usually a temperature below 40 degrees Fahrenheit fish will not be much interested in feeding.

IV. DISEASES OF FISH.

There are many diseases a fish can acquire. Recognition of a diseased condition and treatment is often necessary if the fish is to live.

Identifying a healthy fish is very important. The fish keeper must first be able to identify a healthy fish before a sick fish can be recognized. Since fish come in different sizes and shapes, a few basic observations can be used to identify a healthy fish. The fins usually stand straight out on a healthy fish. They are not frayed or held close to the body of the fish. Healthy fish have bright, clear eyes. There is no discoloration in the appearance of the body.

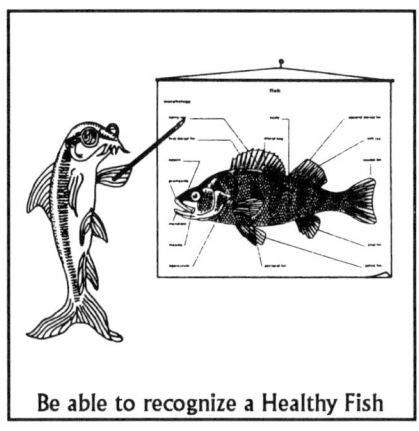

Be able to recognize a Healthy Fish

Many fish diseases are caused by a multitude of opportunistic pathogens. That is, the disease causing agent is often already present in the water garden and awaits for an opportunity to attack the fish. One of these opportunistic times is when the fish is stressed. Stress can be produced by poor nutrition, overcrowding, rough handling or poor water quality. Healthy fish in quality water are less likely to succumb to an opportunistic pathogen. Remember, prevention is much better than a cure.

A few common fish diseases are:

1. **Fish Fungus**. This is recognized by a brown or off-white cotton woolly-like growth on the fins or body of the fish. A fungus cure should be used.

2. **Fish White Spot Disease**. This is recognized by a "salt and pepper" appearance of parasitic white spots on the

body of the fish and is called "**Ich**" (abbreviated for the parasite *Ichthyophthiriasis*). These are the white cysts of the parasite. The fish will appear often listless and rub against rocks. These parasites can often be mistaken for other parasites and a remedy should be used not only for Ich but other parasites such as ciliates, flagellates or trematodes.

3. **Bacterial Infections**. Tail rot, skin ulcers and red wounds usually indicate a bacterial infection. This is a common disease for goldfish and koi and is known as "*furunculosis*" or ulcer disease. Ulcer disease is a systemic (internal) infection caused by a common occurring bacteria found in nature. The infection produces raised boils and small ulcers on the fish. The reason the disease is common is because it is often associated with a stressed fish. A medicated fish food often successfully treats this systemic bacteria.

Many diseases of fish cannot be diagnosed easily. Prevention is better than trying to cure a disease. An excellent general tonic for fish is a prescribed salt treatment used on a regular basis.

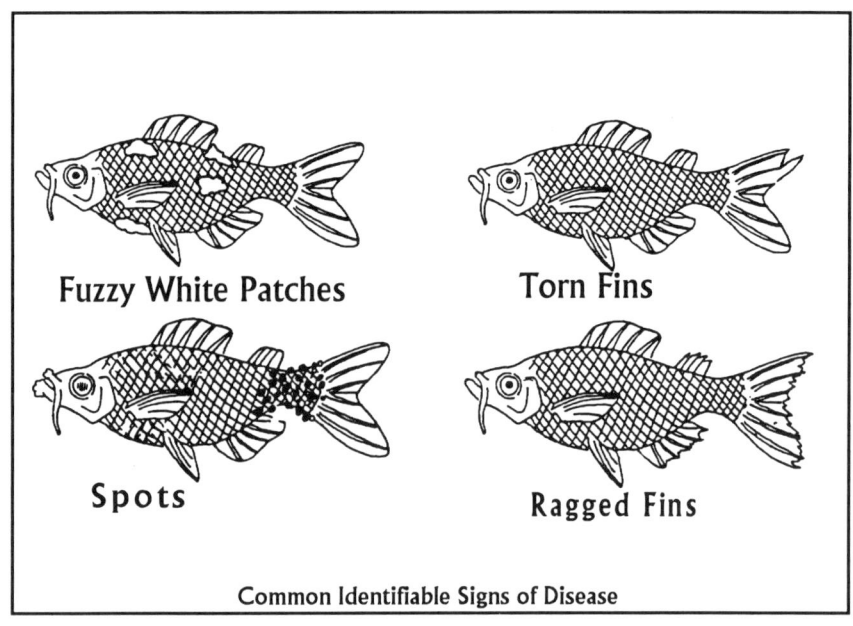

Common Identifiable Signs of Disease

V. ARRIVAL OF FISH FOR THE WATER GARDEN POOL.

Preparation of the Pool for Fish. The water garden pool should have been filled with water at least three days before introducing fish. If chlorinated water has just been added the chlorine should be removed. Chlorine is a gas that can cause severe gill damage which leads to death of the fish dying from asphyxiation. This can be done by the use of an antichlorine chemical remover.

Since fish are shipped in plastic bags they often arrive in a stressed condition. It is this very reason that the water garden pool water must be of good quality. Stress often sets the stage for diseases by lowering the disease resistance of the fish.

As a disease preventative measure, it is highly advisable to treat the water garden pool before the fish arrive. An opportunistic pathogen, such as a bacteria, fungus or parasite can already be present in the water garden pool. Already existing healthy fish in the water garden can be carrying a low grade of pathogens and not show any signs due to their resistance. However, a newly introduced stressed fish can become susceptible to these diseases and succumb to death from the opportunistic pathogen. This in turn can increase the amount of pathogens and begin to effect the healthy fish.

An Ich remedy is most appropriate as a preventative measure before introducing newly arrived fish whether the water garden has a pre-existing population of fish or not.

If fish are already established in the water garden and a new lot of fish are to be added, a quarantine period should be set up for the newly arrived fish. This quarantine involves a "holding tank" of quality water. During this quarantine the fish can be treated with an Ich or bacterial remedy and careful attention to any abnormal behavior can be observed. After a quarantine period of approximately two weeks the fish should no longer be stressed or carry any opportunistic pathogens. They can then be released into the water garden pool with the other fish.

One last consideration of adding fish to a water garden pool with pre-existing fish is to be sure that the water garden does not become over stocked with fish. This will cause stress on the pre-existing fish as well as the new fish. The balanced nitrogen cycle may not be able to handle more fish. A rule of thumb is not to add more than *"one inch of fish* (not including their tails) *to one gallon of water."* This rule has been published by many noted fish experts for decades as a good rule to avoid over crowding. The rule is often based upon fish in a well balanced water garden and consideration of future growth. Pump filtration and other mechanical aids can allow more fish than the standard rule.

Receipt of the Fish. Upon receipt of the fish, remove the plastic bag from the carton and float the plastic bag in the pool for approximately 15 minutes. Fish can not tolerate a rapid change in temperature and can die from a sudden change in temperature. Floating the plastic bag containing the fish will equalize the temperature of the water inside the bag with the water in the pool. This will prevent the temperature shock to the fish.

After floating the plastic bag with fish for 15 minutes, the fish can now be released into the pond.

VI. WINTER CARE OF FISH. If ice is a threat to the water garden, the fish can winter without harm as long as the water garden does not freeze solid and a method is made to allow any noxious gases to escape from under the ice.

Nature has a special way to protect the life of all of her ponds from freezing solid in the winter. As ice freezes it becomes less dense and floats on top of the water garden. This floating ice then becomes an insulator to the water below.

If ice became more dense as it froze and sunk to the bottom of the water garden, it would not be long before all our ponds and water garden pools would freeze solid and aquatic life would cease to exist as we know it.

Once ice is formed at the surface it will trap any noxious gases under the ice. Noxious gases are produced from the decay of plants and other life that is being wintered under the ice. The noxious gases can easily cause fish kills which are common in the spring after a thaw.

To release the noxious gases trapped under the ice in winter a water garden electric pool heater can be used. This is a special electrical device that floats on the surface of the water. At low temperatures of freezing an electrical element turns on and keeps a small hole open in the ice. It is through this small hole that all noxious gases will escape into the atmosphere.

Calico Fantail

CHAPTER 7

SCAVENGERS

Enough cannot be said in favor of scavengers for the water garden pool. Not only do the scavengers provide beauty and charm but they are the housekeepers of the water garden pool. Nature provides scavengers in natural ponds and introduction to the water garden pool is essential.

Our Ecological Friends, the Frogs

I. SNAILS. Snails devour algae and feed on decaying plant vegetation. They also help in cleaning up any excess fish food not consumed by the fish. It is not uncommon to find snails feeding under an old decaying water lily leaf.

The snail population does not get out of hand in an ecologically balanced outdoor water garden. The balanced ecosystem keeps the snail population in control. The adult snails sometimes becomes food for ducks, raccoons and other larger animals. The eggs of newly hatched snails can become food for fish and other aquatic animal life.

It is recommended to add at least **one snail for every one to two square feet of water.** Thus, a water garden 10 feet by 15 feet (150 square feet) should have added at least 15 to 30 snails. Since there are different types of snails with different appetites and functions, a variety of snails for each water garden is recommended:

a. **Trapdoor snails** (*Vivaparus malleatus*) or **Japanese snails** have an unusual "trapdoor" on the bottom of the shell. This trapdoor opens and the movement of the snail becomes evident. Trapdoor snails are often the size of a walnut. They love to move throughout the water garden's bottom and on the aquatic vegetation. They perform as a scavenger admirably.

Trapdoor Snail

b. **Melantho snails** (*Lymnaea sp.*) have an unusual spiral shell. They have a tremendous appetite for decaying leaves, feeding on the decayed leaf and algae.

When dislodged from an aquatic leaf the melantho snail will float upside down on the water surface. In this position two characteristic tentacles can be seen on the body as it slowly moves across the water in search of a stable resting place on some aquatic decaying vegetation.

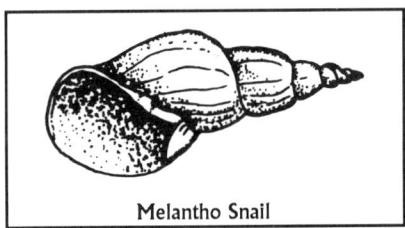
Melantho Snail

c. **Black Ramshorn snails** *(Helisoma sp.)* have a beautiful "ramshorn" or helical shape characteristic of their shell. They commonly are the size of a dime and can grow larger in good conditions. The ramshorn snails are excellent feeders of decayed vegetation and algae.

Ramshorn Snail

d. **Mystery snails** *(Ampullaria* sp.) are the largest of the North American snails, being the size of a large walnut. Most snails lay jelly-like eggs on aquatic vegetation in the water. The mystery snails however come out of the water to lay their cluster of eggs on emerged aquatic stems, such as on the stem of an umbrella palm, taro, etc. Watching the snail lay the cluster (about two inches) of small white eggs is a most unusual and memorable site, nature at its best.

Mystery Snail

Introducing Snails to the Water Garden.

Snails are introduced into the water garden by gently placing them into the water. They will naturally find the best spot in the water garden. The snails usually will sink to the bottom of the water garden pool. If they float, slow movement of the snail will become evident. Slowly the snails will begin to move around exploring the water garden and finding their niche or special spot in the community of aquatic life in the pool. Often the movement is not visible but a trail in the algae or pond debris on the bottom or sides of the pool is identifiable within a few minutes.

II. CLAMS. Freshwater clams or mussels can be considered a small living filter for the water garden. They can make cloudy water sparkling clear. A disturbed clam will close its shell or valve. After the clam is introduced into the water garden the clam will slowly open the shell. It can move by a single "foot", identified by a tongue-like appendage emerging from the clam. If the clam moves, it is very slow. The movement can best be identified by the path left as it moves through the algae and pond debris. It is recommended to add at least a dozen clams to a medium sized pool, approximately 10 by 15 feet. Cloudy water gardens often requires more clams.

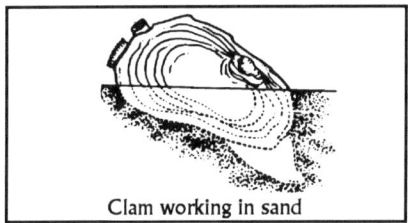
Clam working in sand

III. AMERICAN SALAMANDERS.

Salamanders are tailed amphibians. The American salamander will grow three to four inches in length. Salamanders have a tremendous or voracious appetite for insects. They secret a toxic substance, not detectable to us, through their skin that makes fish and other predators avoid them. Eggs are laid on submerged aquatic vegetation in the late spring or late winter and hatch into the water in late summer or early fall. During winter salamanders hibernate.

A pair of salamanders makes a wonderful addition to any water garden. Introduce the salamanders by gently placing them at the water's edge and they will swim into the water.

American Salamander

IV. TADPOLES.

Tadpoles live on decaying matter and green algae. The tadpole breathes by gills. Once it develops into an adult frog it breathes by lungs and becomes a voracious carnivore feeding primarily on insects, spiders and crustaceans. During the winter frogs will hibernate at the bottom of the water garden. It is recommended to add at least a dozen of tadpoles to a medium sized pool, approximately 10 by 15 feet.

Introduce tadpoles into the water garden similar to adding fish, by first floating the bag for 15 minutes before releasing them. If they come to the surface of the water to gulp air, this is a sign that their lungs are being developed and adulthood as a frog is not far off.

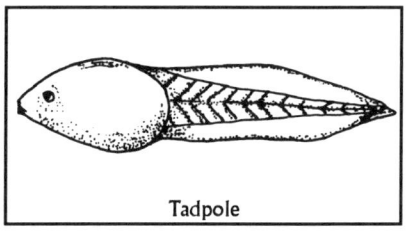
Tadpole

CHAPTER 8

MISCELLANEOUS WATER GARDEN TOPICS:

1. Water Fountains and Cascades.
2. Stray Animals
3. Filters: Biological and Mechanical.
4. Cement Cracks.
5. Overfill Drains.
6. Algae.
7. Fall Preparation.

1. WATER FOUNTAINS AND CASCADES.

The sight and sound of moving water adds a dimension to the water garden that is most pleasing. Adding a water fountain or a water cascade can not only be attractive but keeps the water circulating and adds oxygen. When making a fountain or cascade, a separate area of the water garden should be set aside. Water lilies and other aquatic plants like quiet or undisturbed water.

A. Making a Fountain:

Making a water garden fountain is extremely simple. All one needs is an aquatic pump and a fountain head. Many different variations can be utilized but the fundamentals are presented:

A waterfall added to a special corner of the water garden adds a soothing sound of water that cannot be equaled with any other form of gardening.

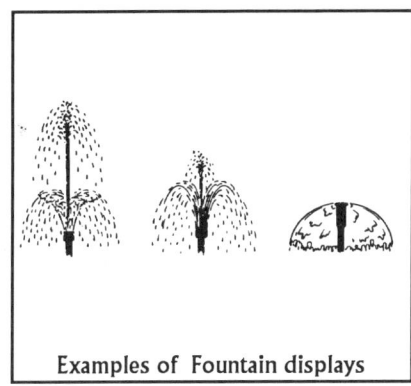

Examples of Fountain displays

B. **Making a Waterfall or Cascade:**

Making a waterfall or cascade is another simple project. All one needs is an aquatic pump, plastic tubing and a water proof cascade or waterfall course. Many variations can be made, however the fundamental idea is discussed:

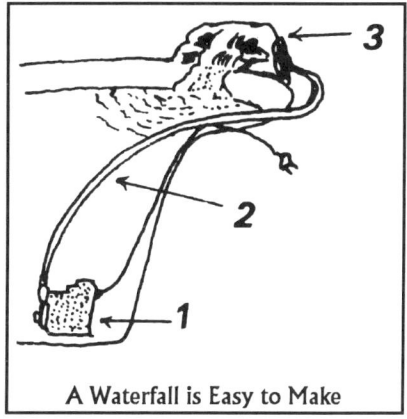

A Waterfall is Easy to Make

(1) **ATTACH THE FOUNTAIN HEAD.** There are many different types of fountain heads to choose. Fountain heads attach directly to the aquatic pump.

(2) **PLACE THE PUMP WITH FOUNTAIN HEAD INTO THE WATER.** The pump is then placed into the water. Support the underside of the pump to allow the fountain head to spray above the water level.

(3) **PLUG IN THE PUMP.** The pump should always be plugged into a **ground fault interrupter**, or **GFI**. A GFI is a special electrical plug that prevents electrocution and should always be used. In the event of a short electrical circuit, the GFI will turn off the electricity to prevent electrical shock.

If debris clogs the pump or fountain head a mechanical filter can be used to screen out such debris.

(1.) **SELECT A PUMP.** Water garden pumps main difference is the amount of gallons of water pumped at specific heights. Some pumps are designed to be placed directly into the water and others can operate out of the water. In the above drawing, the pump selected is submerged in the water garden. When plugging in the pump, a ground fault interrupter, GFI, should be used.

(2) **ATTACH THE TUBING TO THE PUMP.** Attach the tubing to the out put of the aquatic pump. The length

57

of the tubing depends on the location of the pump and the distance to the water fall or water course.

(3) **THE WATERFALL COURSE.** The waterfall course must be water proof, that is, the water as it flows over or down the cascade must not be made of soil or other porous material. Soil or other porous material will absorb water and eventually drain the water garden. The plastic tubing is then secured behind or at the top of the water course or waterfall. After everything is attached, the cascade or waterfall should flow wonderfully.

During operation of the waterfall or cascade there will be some evaporation. However, if too much water is added to the water garden periodically the cascade or waterfall should be checked for leaks.

The waterfall or cascade can be a preformed watercourse or a piece of rubber lining material which are water proof. If using a lining material for the water course, add a few rocks to give a realistic effect. Be careful not to use limestone and other rocks that can leach chemicals and change the quality of the water.

If the flow of the water is too great, a water restrictor clamp can be used on the plastic tubing to restrict the flow of water.

2. **STRAY ANIMALS.**

Stray animals that are attracted to the pond such as raccoons can be discouraged. Animal deterrent kits are available which consists of a set of small posts with a wire that carries a small electrical charge similar to a miniature electrical horse fence. Once the pest learns of the fence by a mild and memorable shock, the fence can be removed.

3. **FILTERS...BIOLOGICAL and MECHANICAL.**

There are two types of water garden filters: **biological** and **mechanical filters**. The biological filters, discussed in the chapter on fish, provide an environment for bacteria to grow and help to ecologically balance the water. The mechanical filters are used in conjunction with water garden pumps and fountain heads to help filter small particles that may clog the fountain head.

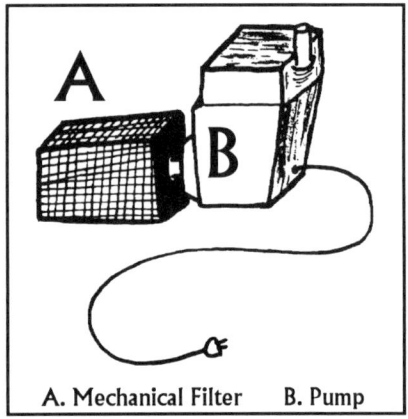

A. Mechanical Filter   B. Pump

4. **CEMENT CRACKS.**

Cracks in the concrete of the water

garden can be repaired. If there is a large crack, ie. large enough to slide the head of a screwdriver into, the use of a "plugging" cement product can be used. The cement plugging products can physically stop a flowing water leak. The crack is prepared by chipping away excess concrete and using a wire brush to expose the bare concrete. In addition, there are also chemical "binders" that can be mixed into the cement plugging compounds to get better adhesion. After the cracks are repaired, the entire concrete pond can be painted with a clear liquid sealer.

Smaller cracks can be repaired by using a cement sealing compound. The entire concrete area must be prepared by cleaning with a wire brush. The sealing compound is a cement product that is mixed with water and applied to the prepared surface using a coarse brush.

If concrete repair becomes too familiar every year, it would be recommended to line the entire pond with a rubber liner to stop all leaks.

5. AN OVERFILL DRAIN.

Bulk Head Fittings can be used for overfill drains in the water garden. Simply make the correct size of hole in the liner or preformed pool and attach by screwing in the bulk head fitting. After the bulk head fitting is installed, PVC fittings can be adapted to extend the drain.

6. ALGAE.

Algae, a primitive plant, is a part of the ecologically balanced water garden and can grow rapidly under certain circumstances.

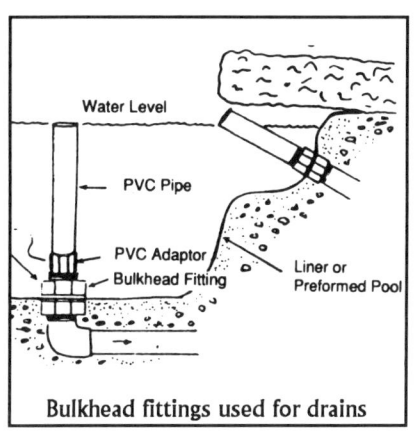

Bulkhead fittings used for drains

Algae is not necessarily the enemy of the water garden. It, like the oxygenators, produces oxygen for the water garden and is part of the complicated food chain existing in nature. Too much algae, however, becomes unsightly and indicates that the water garden in not balanced and begins to upset the ecology of the water garden, referred to as *algal blooms*.

In an algal bloom, the oxygen level in the pond is reduced drastically at night when the algae stops producing oxygen and continues to release carbon dioxide. This reduction in oxygen can severely effect the aquatic animals, such as fish.

Since algae can grow rapidly, algal booms can occur naturally as the water garden begins in the spring. As the water garden becomes established with other plants it can naturally balance and control the algae. However, algae can flourish on excess fertilizer, excess fish food, decaying plants, fish wastes etc., and cause algal blooms throughout the summer months.

Biological control is the best solution to reduce algae. This can be done by covering 60 to 70 percent of the surface of the water with aquatic plants which will subsequently reduce the sunlight that is necessary for rapid algal growth. Also, the aquatic plants compete with the algae by taking out minerals faster than the algae. This results in the starvation of the algae. One of best aquatic plants that compete with algae is the floating water hyacinth.

7. FALL PREPARATION.

In autumn, leaves from trees can enter the water garden. Using a net covering over the water garden pool in autumn will prevent the leaves from entering. After the leaves have dropped, the net covering can be removed.

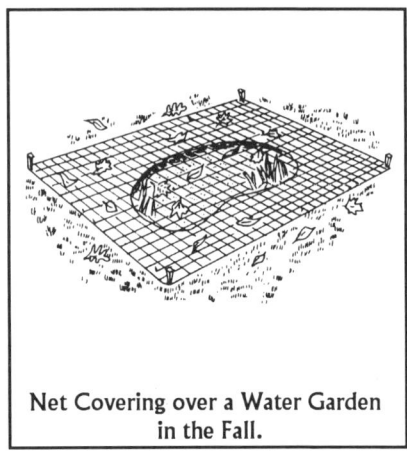

Net Covering over a Water Garden in the Fall.

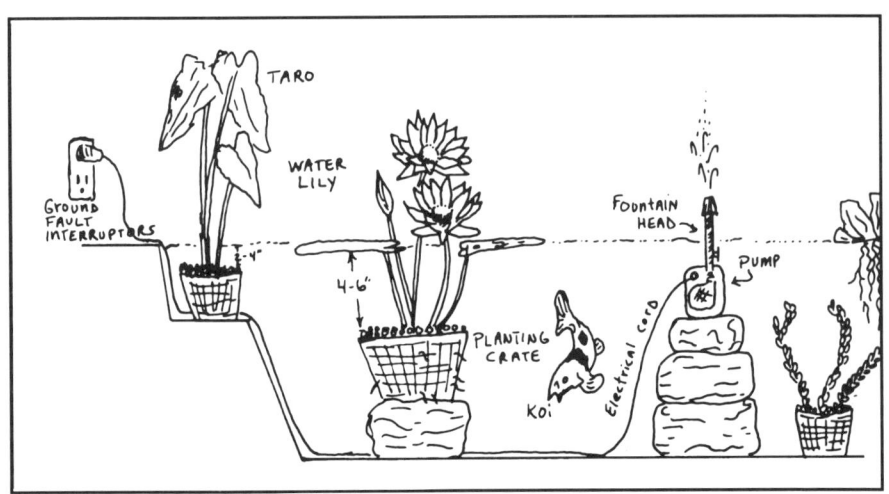

CHAPTER 9

ARRANGING the WATER PLANTS in the POOL and TUB GARDENS

Planting the water garden pool can be exciting with all of the aquatic plants to choose from. There are no set rules to follow in selecting and arranging water plants in the pool. Some individuals prefer to have a dense cover of aquatics, while others save room on the water's surface to reflect the sky and images of the water lilies and other tall aquatic plants.

Examples of how arrangements are made can give an idea of the many different plantings that can be used:

I. Medium Size Pool

A medium size circular pool, seven or eight feet across or a rectangular pool of the approximate dimensions of six by eight foot, the following can be planted as indicated:

A. Four water lilies, any preference can be made. A tropical night blooming water lily with a day blooming water lily will give 24 hours of blooms.

B. Shallow water plants such as *Papyrus* and *Arrowhead* are ideal for a centerpiece.

I. Medium Size Pool

C. Aquatic plants: Lower right corner, three *Yellow Iris* and *Radican*. Upper right hand corner, two *Taros* and an *Umbrella Palm*. Upper left hand corner, two *Taros* and an *Umbrella Palm*. Lower left hand corner, two *Pickerel Rush* and a *Dwarf Sweet Flag*.

D. For planting beneath the surface in submerged planting containers (not shown) could be five oxygenating plants such as *Anacharis, Cabomba, Vallisneria, Green Hygrophilia*, etc.

E. Two floating plants such as *Water Hyacinth* and *Water lettuce*.

II. **Small Size Pool**: In a small rectangular pool of four by six or five by seven feet the following can be represented:

A. Three potted lilies, may be a hardy, a day blooming tropical and a night blooming lily which would make 24 hours of blooms.

B. A centerpiece planting of shallow water plants, *Papyrus* and *Pickerel Rush* or *Arrowhead*.

C. Lower right hand corner, *Parrot Feather* and *Dwarf Papyrus*. Upper Right hand corner, *Hardy Thalia, Forget-me-not* and *Primrose Creeper*. Upper Left hand corner, *Taro's*. Lower Left hand corner, *Yellow* or *Blue Iris* and *Floating Heart*.

II. Small Size Pool

D. Floating plant, *Water Hyacinth*.

E. Oxygenating Plants (not shown) can be submerged such as *Anarcharis*, *Milfoil*, etc.

III. Rectangular Pool

A rectangular pool, approximate 10 feet by 15 feet, planting as drawn:

A through H. Eight water lilies, many choices and color schemes can be used.

I. Centerpiece: Shown are lotus plants with a grouping of *Papyrus* plants surrounding the *Lotus*.

J. Corner with a *Taro* and *Dwarf Papyrus*.

K. Corner with *Flowering Rush* and *Pickerel Rush*.

III. Rectangular Pool

L. Corner with a *Floating Heart*, *Green Taro* and *Papyrus*.

M. Corner with *Pickerel Rush*, *Parrot Feather* and *Giant Arrowhead*.

Floating Plant, *Water Hyacinth* (next to G water lily) gives a graceful, quiet appearance.

Oxygenating Plants (not shown, but planted in the depths) can be *Anacharis*, *Cabomba*, etc.

IV. A Water Garden Planting

On the following page is a photograph of a water garden that was proudly displayed in William Tricker, Inc.'s 1928 mail order catalog. The same pride can be achieved with similar plantings as a guideline. Corresponding with the numbers in the outline of this water garden, the following plants are identified:

1. **Lotus.** This wonderful plant can be admired from the edge of the water garden. The location of the lotus will allow any admirer to smell the mysterious fragrance of the flower.

2. **Umbrella Palm.** This plant adds height and fullness to balance the lotus. A gentle breeze will make the foliage rustle ever so gently.

3. **Blue Beauty Water Lily.** This tropical water lily, with five blooms, has a wonderful spicy flower. It will continue to bloom profusely throughout the summer.

4. **Gloriosa Water Lily.** This hardy water lily will give a glorious red color reflection in the water and can be seen from a distant.

5. **General Pershing Water Lily.** This tropical water lily has wonderful pink flowers. The leaves or lily pads have a beautiful olive color with small maroon dashes on them.

6. **Reflecting Water.** In many water gardens it is hard to omit a space for reflection of the plants and sky. These mirror reflections are important since they can not be seen in any other type of gardening.

7. **Roses.** Roses can complement any water garden. Some water gardeners plant the roses close enough to see their reflection in the water pool.

8. **Deciduous hedges.** These hedges or plantings enclose the area to make the water garden a focal place. Often these hedges follow or complement the contour of the water garden edge.

9. **Floating Water Plants.** These plants will float on the surface to bring an interesting display of color and admiration at one end of the lily pool. The floating plants can be *Shell Flower*, *Water Hyacinths*, *Floating Fern* or *Azolla*.

IV. A Water Garden Planting

Outline of Photograph above. Plant Key on previous page.

V. TUB WATER GARDENS.

No garden is too large or too small for a tub garden. Water lilies and aquatics will thrive and blossom in a container as small as a tub. A tub garden is a complete water garden in miniature. And like a miniature painting, it may have an individuality of color and beauty that makes it delightful and desirable as a garden on a grander scale.

A water leak proof container is all that is necessary for a tub garden. Whiskey barrels (lined with a pond liner, since they may leak or leach residual chemicals that may be toxic to plants or fish) or a prefabricated polyethylene tubs can be used.

Choose a sunny location such as a sun porch, patio or a special location in the yard. The tub can either be set on the ground or sunk into the ground. If sunk in the ground, rock plants and a margin of rocks can be used for a border.

No pool, even if it is a miniature, is complete without a few ornamental fish. Goldfish illuminate the water with flashes of red-gold. A few fishes put in spring may give enough fish to stock a good sized indoor aquarium by fall.

Sunken Tub Garden. (see below)

1. Rock Plants or Perennials.
2. Rocks.
3. Giant Arrowhead.
4. Water Lily.
5. Water Hyacinth.
6. Umbrella Palm.
7. Shell Flower or Water Lettuce.
8. Snails.
9. Oxygenating Plants.

The aquatic plants can be either planted in containers or soil can be added to the entire tub.

Tub Garden's are easy to make and will be enjoyed by all

The above drawing is a tub garden with potted plants: *Dwarf Papyrus, Tropical Water Lily* and a *Water Poppy.*

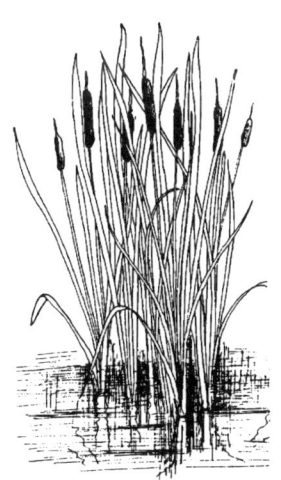

William Tricker, Inc. offers a full color mail order catalog of the aquatic plants and supplies discussed in this book. A catalog can be ordered for a nominal fee from:

William Tricker, Inc.
7125 Tanglewood Drive
Independence, Ohio 44131

(216) 524-3491